Noel Rochford
John and Pat Underwood

walk & eat
CORSICA

walk & eat **CORSICA**

CONTENTS

PLANS OF BASTIA AND AJACCIO	*inside front cover*
INTRODUCTION	4
the walks	5
the railway excursion	5
the restaurants	6
the recipes	6
corsican food	7
corsican wines	9
planning your visit	11
when to go	11
where to stay	12
what to take	12
planning your walks	13
on arrival	14
information	14
shopping for self-catering	14
WALK 1 • bonifacio	16
restaurant: u castille	23
recipes: stuffed aubergines bonifacio-style, omelette with *brocciu*	24
WALK 2 • forêt de l'ospédale	26
restaurant: le refuge	31
recipes: fig chutney, wild boar stew with ceps	32
WALK 3 • trou de la bombe	38
restaurant: auberge du col de bavella	39
recipes: veal cutlets with honey sauce, chestnut tart	40
WALK 4 • pointe de la parata	42
restaurant: le weekend	46
recipe: courgette fritters	47
WALK 5 • cascades des anglais	48
restaurant: hôtel du monte d'oro	54
recipes: duck breast with honey sauce, trout with pine nuts	56
WALK 6 • the venacos	58
restaurants: le torrent and bar/restaurant de la place	64
recipes: chicken in curry and coconut milk, vegetable 'cake'	66

contents

WALK 7 • la restonica 68
restaurant: auberge de la restonica 73
recipes: roast leg of lamb with garlic, grilled sea bass with fennel 74

WALK 8 • cascades d'aitone 76
restaurant: hôtel l'aitone 80
recipes: rabbit sautéed with ceps 81

WALK 9 • sentier du littoral 82
restaurant: l'olivier 87
recipes: two ways with mussels, 'petit Napoléon' 88

WALK 10 • ostriconi 90
restaurant: village de l'ostriconi 93

WALK 11 • notre-dame de la serra 94
restaurant: u fanale 99
restaurants: u casanu, le comme chez soi 100
recipe: traditional corsican soup 102
recipes: meat stew with smoked ham, *salade bergère* . 103
recipes: *langoustine* risotto, pork and chestnut terrine ... 104

WALK 12 • lumio, occi and lavatoggio 106
refreshments/restaurant: juste pour m and chez edgard . 111
recipe: seafood salad with a citrus vinaigrette 112
recipe: veal sauté with prunes and figs 112

WALK 13 • sant' antonino and l'île-rousse 114
refreshments/restaurant: cave à citron and la cave . 121
recipes: chestnut cake, *fiadone* 123

EXCURSION • 'u trinichellu' 124
ISLAND MAP (excluding cap corse) 126
recipes: braised endives with *panzetta*, beans corsican-style ... 130
recipe: chestnut sauerkraut with chestnut beer 131

TRANSPORT 132

EAT GF, DF 134
eating in restaurants 135
self-catering 136
   gf, df shopping 136
   gf, df cooking; conversion tables 138

GLOSSARY (menu items, shopping terms) 139

INDEX 141

IN THE RESTAURANT (pocket vocabulary) ..... *inside back cover*

This pocket guide is designed for visitors to the island who would like to do some fairly easy walking as opposed to tackling the more difficult routes. This may be because it's too hot in high season, or you are travelling with children.

We've hand-picked enough walks, restaurants and recipes to fill a week wherever you are based although, since Corsica is such a large island, not all will be right on your doorstep!

The highlights at a glance:
- 13 varied day walks, each with topographical map
- 1 excursion — on the world-famous 'Trinichellu', Corsica's narrow-gauge railway
- recommended restaurants
- recipes to make at your self-catering base or back home
- special section with hints on wheat-, gluten- and dairy-free eating and cooking on the island

INTRO

THE WALKS

The walks in this book (a baker's dozen') range from easy, flat routes along the coast to fairly gentle hillside hikes. Dotted round the island (see map on page 126), they have been chosen for their magnificent views or natural surroundings, *with the added bonus of a good restaurant nearby*. Special emphasis has also been placed on restaurants that are open outside the peak summer season. For a wide selecion of island walks, we recommend Noel Rochford's *Landscapes of Corsica*, with 70 long and short walks. It's one of Sunflower's 'Landscapes' guides, a series featuring walks and car tours for some 50 destinations. For more information see www.sunflowerbooks.co.uk.

> Authors' note
> As publishers at Sunflower, we got to know this wonderful island many years ago, when following the walks in Noel Rochford's guide, *Landscapes of Corsica*. So this book is a three-way effort: Noel contributed most of the walks, with the two of us adding walks over the years.
> ... as well as doing most of the eating and cooking ...
> — John and Pat Underwood

THE RAILWAY EXCURSION

A 'day out' on Corsica's narrow-gauge railway is *not to be missed*. The journey is an excursion in itself — and all the better when combined with a meal at one of the restaurants we recommend — but you can also combine the trip with a short walk.

The train can also be used to reach other walks in the book. The main line runs between Ajaccio and Bastia, with connections from Calvi and l'Ile-Rousse. The whole trip is rather long, so we have suggested a shorter version depending on where you are based. But many people like to do the entire route; if so, plan to stay overnight at one end.

THE RESTAURANTS

We have *featured* the restaurants we use regularly (or have just discovered) and say why we like them. In each case we include a 'mini-menu' listing some of their specialities. A price guide is given (€ to €€€) to indicate 'very reasonable' to 'fairly pricey'. But remember that you can have a relatively inexpensive meal in a five-star establishment if you just have a light lunch — for instance Corsican soup or the famous omelette with *brocciu*.

No restaurant has paid — in cash or in kind — to be included in this guide.

Some of the restaurants, especially those in the mountains, are at hotels where you might like to spend the night, especially if you want to have dinner there and there is no public transport back to base later in the evening.

THE RECIPES

Most of our recommended restaurants were willing to share with us the main *ingredients* used in their recipes, but the actual preparation remains their closely guarded secret. We gathered as much information as possible and then cooked all the dishes ourselves, to make sure they 'work' and are at least a fair approximation of the restaurant's version.

The recipes selected have been chosen to offer as wide a

spectrum of dishes as possible. What we cannot guarantee, of course, is that they will taste as good back home as they did on Corsica! So many factors come into play to make food taste better when you are on holiday — from the intangibles (the atmosphere and the sense of relaxation after a day's good walking) to the tangible (wild boar and *brocciu* are a little hard to come by back home!). So if you are in self-catering, why not try some of these recipes while you're on the island?

It's very unlikely that you will come face-to-face with any wild boars on the walks in *this* book, but you *will* see them by the roadside, snaffling the chestnuts, mushrooms and nuts that impart such a rich flavour to their meats, whether roasted or smoked.

We've made all of these dishes on the simple kind of cooker usually found in self-catering (a decent oven is a *must*) — or on a barbecue. And good news for anyone suffering food intolerances: all of the recipes can be **gluten- and dairy-free** (see page 134).

CORSICAN FOOD

Aside from the few times when we've just fancied the local grilled fish, we have always opted for the regional dishes, variously called *menu corse, menu du terroir,* etc.

walk & eat **CORSICA**

Assiette régionale at the Auberge de la Restonica — a work of art, with (clockwise from the bottom): *coppa* (smoked pork fillet), pork terrine and smoked sausage, *lonzu* (smoked pork shoulder), *prizuttu* (prosciutto), olives, pickles and chutney

Top of our list would be the **mixed plate of local meats** (see left). (Another meat speciality, not shown, is *figatellu*, a sausage of pork liver and offal usually served fried or grilled on a wood fire.) **Soups** are a must, from the famous *suppa corsa* (recipe page 102) to fresh soup of Corsican rock fish served with *rouille* (orange-coloured mayonnaise of olive oil, garlic, peppers and saffron).

For a light meal there are omelettes, especially the *omelette au brocciu* (an ewes'-milk cheese similar to ricotta), seasoned with mint (recipe page 25). Other possibilites include endless **pasta** dishes, sometimes with a sauce of fish or seafood, **pizzas** of all descriptions, **mussels** *(moules)* in a variety of sauces. Another tasty dish is a plate of **fritters** *(beignets)* — usually aubergines or courgettes (recipe page 47) or **stuffed aubergines** (recipe page 24), always served with a tomato sauce.

Down on the coast, the **fish and seafood** is out of this world (if fairly pricey). There is an enormous selection, and the restaurant will usually either grill it, or fry or poach and then sauce it in many different ways. While fish is usually *presented* whole (as

introduction

> ### Corsican wines
> Corsica has produced wine since Greek and Roman times; most are strong and full-bodied with a fruity bouquet. We have only had two poor wines — both white and from the southeast. The best wines are produced in Appellation d'Origine Contrôlée areas: Ajaccio, Calvi (Balagne), Côteaux du Cap Corse, Muscat du Cap Corse, Figari, Patrimonio (Nebbiu), Porto-Vecchio and Sartène. All supermarkets stock good Corsican (and French) wines; *Corsican wine is quite pricey.* Some of our favourites include
> *white:* Patrimonio (Nielluccia, Montenagni, both dry), Muscat de Cap Corse
> *rosé:* Clos Landry (Calvi) and those from Cap Corse, Patrimonio and Porto-Vecchio, also Domaine Vico (from Ponte Leccia)
> *red:* Ajaccio (I Peri), Calvi (Domaine Orsini), Figari (Costa Rossa, Petra Bianca), Patrimonio (Clos de Bernardi and Clos Teddi), Domaine Vico (from Ponte Leccia)
> *desert wines:* many are available — try the fruit or herb flavour that appeals!

in the photograph on page 75), it is then removed for filleting if you wish (see page 23). On the other hand, do *not* expect to find a selection of fish dishes up in the mountains … except for the fresh river trout which abounds at places like Vizzavona and Evisa (see recipe on page 57).

While you can get a good steak almost anywhere, more interesting **meats** are to be found in the mountains. Chief among them is **wild boar**, usually served in a stew *(civet de sanglier).* **Veal** is another Corsican speciality, but you may not recognise it. Corsican cattle are raised in the open, not confined to pens. The cuts are thicker and more like pork in colour, and the taste is very different from what you may be used to, since the cattle are free-range and graze. **Lamb**, often on the menu as 'milk-fed lamb' *(agneau de lait)* can be a mixed bag in our experience; it certainly did not equate to suckling or baby lamb in any restaurant we visited and was sometimes mutton-like, strongly flavoured but very tender, with quite a lot of fat. **Baby goat** and **suckling pig** also figure on some menus; as well as **rabbit** and **game** (in the mid-August to December hunting season). Virtually all meats come in a hearty sauce, usually a reduction of red wine, seasoned with herbs of the *maquis* — thyme, rosemary, fennel, sage, majoram, juniper, mint and *nepita* (peppery 'Corsican marjoram'). Sometimes olives are added.

Pasta is the carbohydrate of choice with most meat dishes and rice with fish, but virtually all restaurants also have potatoes … and many serve another Corsican speciality, *polenta*. This is sometimes made in the usual way, with corn meal (and may be fried), sometimes with chestnut flour (resulting in a much darker colour).

Corsican **cheeses** are produced from goats' and ewes' milk and vary from fresh (mild and creamy) to really strong matured cheeses. *Brocciu* (from ewes' milk) is the most popular; it is quite like ricotta, and is used in many savoury and sweet recipes. In the shops you'll see a lot of *tomme* cheeses: made from goats' milk, these are not native to Corsica but have become popular in recent years. Fresh figs or fig chutney (recipe page 32) are often served with the cheese course.

We often give **sweet** courses a miss, but less so on Corsica. Almost every restaurant with a regional menu features some version of **chestnut cake**, and at many restaurants this is 100% chestnut flour. At the Auberge du Col de Bavella they do a chestnut tart (our version on page 41) which they claim is unique on the island. Then there is *fiadone*, a cake made from *brocciu* flavoured with lemon (recipe page 123). But perhaps our favourite dessert of all was the 'Little Napoléon' we enjoyed at a restaurant in St-Florent, for which we give our version on page 89.

And finally: most restaurant portions (especially in the mountains) are *huge*. They didn't mind us sharing a main course, once we told them we wanted to sample as much as possible and could not handle two full 'menus'.

PLANNING YOUR VISIT
When to go
Most people go to Corsica in summer (June to August). Since it can be very hot then (sometimes even 40°C or higher), we've selected quite easy walks, some with an opportunity to swim, others in shady woods. But if you are not tied to school holidays or overly keen on swimming, then *do* consider going outside the main season; charter flights are available from Easter until early November, and we have specifically recommended restaurants that are open in the 'shoulder' months.

If this book gives you a taste of walking on the island and you want to do more, then without doubt the best walking months are from Easter to May or early June and September and October. You may have to put up with a little rain, but really in high summer it's too hot for strenuous hikes. The rates for accommodation outside July and August are also far more reasonable than in high season.

Where to stay

Corsica is a huge island. If you are not renting a car, it is imperative that you stay as near as possible to the centre of one of the four main tourist bases: **Ajaccio/Porto, Calvi, Bastia** and **Porto-Vecchio**. All of these have a wide range of accommodation, from hotels to villas to camping sites. Ajaccio, Calvi and Bastia are on both rail and bus lines. Porto-Vecchio is only served by bus: there *are* connections to far-flung places, but you'll have to get up at the crack of dawn. And beware of Porto: bus connections are very limited and the surrounding roads very slow-going.

Even *with* a car, don't expect to see the whole the island on one visit; it will be enough to get to grips with the region around your base and a trip or two into the mountains. And if you are renting a countryside villa, with car, look at a good map before you choose, remembering that you won't average much more than 25-30km/h on any but the major roads.

What to take

Pack simply! You won't have to 'dress', even for dinner. Instead, concentrate on a (very) few essentials for the walks. While walking boots are recommended for one or two of the walks, they are not essential; just be sure to take some **strong lace-up shoes** with ankle support and good grip. Carry a **small rucksack**, *always* stocked with a **first-aid kit**, **drinks**, **snacks** and a **mobile or smartphone** (the **emergency** number on Corsica, as throughout the EU, is 112). For shadeless beach/seaside walks, add **sun protection** (hat, glasses, cream, full-length cover-ups) and **bathing things**. For walks in the mountains, add **warm clothing**, **long trousers**, **spare socks** and — depending on the season, **windproof**, **lightweight rainwear**, **fleece** and **gloves**.

Note: Mineral water is sold almost everywhere in half-litre bottles; *it is imperative that each walker carries at least a half-litre of water — a full litre in warmer weather.*

Planning your walks

Wherever possible, we have chosen walks where you have the option of using **public transport** ... so that you can enjoy a bottle of wine with lunch! Unfortunately this is not always possible on Corsica. If you hire a **car**, and the route is linear, you can sometimes leave your car at the end of the walk and take a bus or train to the start; otherwise the only option is a taxi.

We have **graded our walks** for the deskbound person who nevertheless keeps reasonably fit. Only one of these walks ascends more than 300m/1000ft, most even less. It is important to remember that the times indicated are *neat point-to-point and do not allow for any stops*; please ***allow up to double the time shown*** to take into account stops for photography and nature-watching — to say nothing of having a meal!

Our walking **maps** are based on the IGN 'Top 25' (1:25,000) series and our own GPS work on the ground. (Free **GPS track** downloads are available for all these walks: see the *Walk & eat Corsica* page on the Sunflower website.) Should you wish to go further afield, the IGN 'Top 25' maps are available everywhere on Corsica, and we give you the number of the relevant sheet at the beginning of each walk. *Even if you don't use GPS,* you should be able to compare our maps with Google Maps on your smartphone and pinpoint your exact position.

Walking safely depends in great part on *knowing what to expect and being properly equipped*. For this reason we urge you to read through the *whole* walk description at your leisure *before* setting out, so that you have a mental picture of each stage of the route and the landmarks. Most of the routes are **signposted** or **waymarked**, and on *most* of these walks you will encounter other people — an advantage if you get into difficulty. Nevertheless, we advise you **never** to walk alone.

ON ARRIVAL
Information
Do call at the nearest tourist office soon after arrival. They can give you information about what's on, and *usually* bus and train timetables. Even if you don't think you will be using the train, it's a good idea to stop at a railway station as well, for up-to-date timetables and information about passes — unless you have already dealt with all that on the web (cf-corse.corsica).

Shopping for self-catering
Although you will no doubt want to visit some local markets, farmers and vintners later, make your first port of call the nearest **supermarket**, not only to stock up on essentials, but local specialities as well. The supermarkets on the island are

introduction

Corsican smoked meats (right) and the fish counter (below) at a supermarket in Calvi: *prices have changed!*

amazingly well stocked with high-quality produce.

All have separate sections for delicatessen items, fishmongers and butchers, as well as bakeries. There are also separate 'kiosks' with regional specialities. Just look at this fish and seafood display at the Casino in Calvi! Most supermarkets open on Sundays; some close for the mid-day break. Aside from staples, you may want to pick up a few extra things that might be missing from your base — like a vegetable peeler or whisk.

Note: *On Corsica plastic carrier bags have never been an option. So bring your own bag or expect to pay for any carriers.*

<u>Supermarket</u>
 <u>shopping list</u>
 <u>reminder</u>
washing-up liquid
 or dishwasher
 tablets
paper towels
aluminium foil
soap
tissues/toilet
 paper
scouring pads
salt & pepper
mineral water
milk/cream*
coffee/tea/
 drinking
 chocolate
butter*

sugar
bread*
juice
wine/beer/cider
olive oil & vinegar
eggs
tomato purée
rice
mayonnaise/
 mustard
batteries?
vegetable peeler?
whisk?

*for gluten- and dairy-free alternatives see pages 136-8

Bonifacio, on the southernmost tip of the island, is a must. This dramatically-sited, cliff-hanging town, with its centuries-old narrow streets, is most impressive. Work up an appetite by taking this walk along the windswept cliff-tops, dazzled by the chalk-white limestone bluffs and the sparkling navy blue sea.

bonifacio
WALK

Begin the walk at the church of **St-Erasme** (**❶**), near the western end of the marina-side cafés in **Bonifacio**. (In the Genoese era this was the fishermen's church, since they were forbidden entry into the town.) Climb the flight of steps (**Montée Rastello**) towards the old town. Tall, ancient buildings (with face-lifts) line the steep pedestrian way. The imposing citadel walls rise high above you, on your right. Five minutes up, a magnificent view awaits you at the **Col St-Roch** (**❷**). You look along the sheer curving coastline of brilliant white cliffs. On clear days you can see the low hills of Sardinia

> **Distance:** 9km/5.6mi; 3h10min
> **Grade:** easy; a walk for all the family. Overall ascents/descents of about 300m/1000ft. Can be very windy: on such days *do not* venture near the edge of the cliff! *Almost no shade.* IGN map 4255 OT
> **Equipment:** see page 12; stout shoes, bathing things, sun protection and plenty of water recommended
> **Transport:** 🚗 to/from Bonifacio (park by the port). Or 🚌 (see page 132); there are buses from both Ajaccio and Porto-Vecchio.
> **Refreshments:**
> bar-cafés, pizzerias, restaurants in Bonifacio; *seasonal* kiosk on the D260
> **Points of Interest:**
> Bonifacio, with a wealth of historical sites and tourist attractions
> cliff formations and coastal flora
> old fortifications
> Capo Pertusato

rising in the southeast. The chapel here at the viewpoint marks the site of the death of the last victim of the Great Plague of 1528, which wiped out 60 per cent of the town's population.

To head out around the cliffs, climb the paved path that ascends to the left ('**Circuit Pedestre des Falaises**'). You have a fine view back towards the strategically-sited town and over into the inlet sheltering the port. Once on the cliffs, hold onto

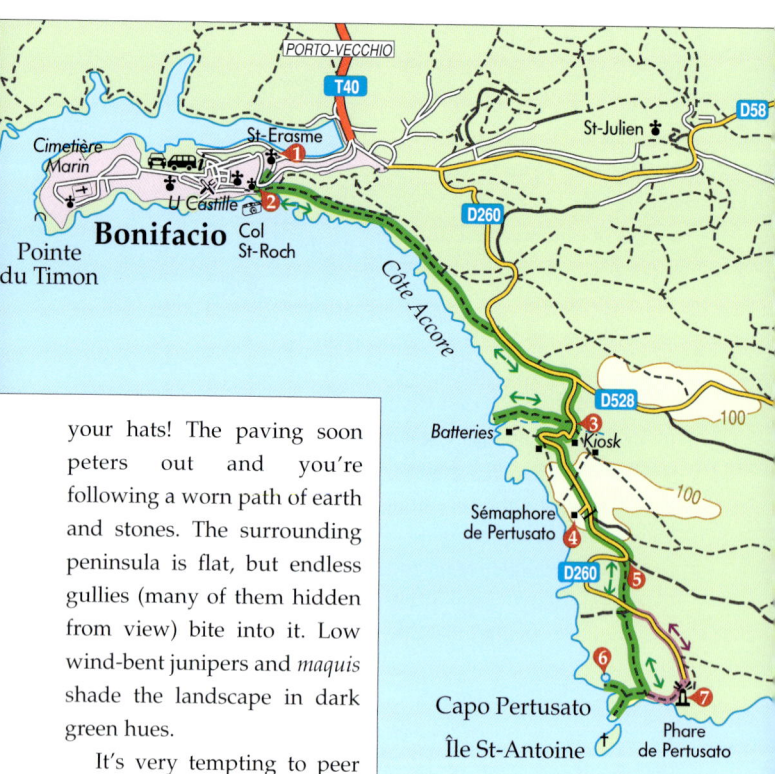

your hats! The paving soon peters out and you're following a worn path of earth and stones. The surrounding peninsula is flat, but endless gullies (many of them hidden from view) bite into it. Low wind-bent junipers and *maquis* shade the landscape in dark green hues.

It's very tempting to peer over the very edge of the cliffs, but *this is exceedingly dangerous*, because there's often a big overhang that could easily crumble away. There are a couple of viewpoints with protective walls; otherwise, keep well back from the edge if it's windy, and supervise children carefully. All

Capo Pertusato: this monumental salient of rock blocks views to the Île St-Antoine and the lighthouse.

the way along you overlook the wind- and sea-eroded coastline — just magnificent!

You pass the **shell of a building** (**30min**) and fifteen minutes later join the **lighthouse road** (**45min**). Turn right here and, when the road forks by a car park on the left with a *seasonal* kiosk (**55min**), head right towards 'Pertusato' beside a sign, 'I Bucchi di Bunifaziu'. Minutes later you circle a small gully. Strike off **right here on a path** (❸); it takes you down to the edge of the sea in eight minutes, onto smooth white tongues of limestone.

Take the same path back to the road and ascend past **gun batteries** and, a little further on, the **Sémaphore de Pertusato**

walk & eat **CORSICA**

At the start of the walk you will see a solitary stack just off the coast. Called the 'Grain du Sable' (Grain of Sand), it is one of Bonifacio's best-known motifs. It would have been part of the limestone cliffs 1000 years ago.

(**4**). Crossing a crest, you get a closer look at Sardinia, only twelve kilometres away. The Iles Lavezzi form the necklace of rocky islets between the two islands; they are part of a protected marine park in the straits. The lighthouse sits alone on the point ahead.

Two or three minutes below the crest, just as the road makes a U-turn, ignore a track going almost straight ahead. But, just 20m/yds further on, take a **path off left** (**5**), ascending through the hillside scrub. Squeezing through the thorny *maquis*, you'll see a wealth of rosemary and red-berried *Lentiscus*. Should you venture upon herds of grazing goats out here, pass them quietly. Five minutes through the scrub you rejoin the road. Turn left and, after 30m/yds, turn hard back to the right on a dirt track. Then, just 40m/yds down the track, take the path descending the left-hand wall of a gully that cuts down to the shore. A curious piece of coastline eaten away by wind and water awaits you. A monumental salient of limestone dominates the hilly waterfront.

When you reach the water's edge, you discover a small sandy **beach** (**1h30min**), obscured by the rocky shoreline. The small islet of Ile St-Antoine, adorned with a cross, hides behind the monumental rock. Climb the rock for another fine view of Bonifacio. A **blowhole** (**6**) lies unnoticed to the right of the rock. Approach the edge with the utmost care, as it, too, is eaten away underneath. Pay particular attention when gale force winds batter the point here!

You may want to visit the lighthouse (**Phare de Pertusato**; **7**), which lies a few minutes along the road to the right (time not included in the main walk).

Otherwise, return the same way to Bonifacio. In calm weather, you may want to explore some paths to the left of the road, along the shoreline.

Once back at the **Col St-Roch** (**2**; **3h10min**), rather than descending Montée Rastello, you could take **Montée St-Roch** to the old town ('haute ville'), where you can call at the tourist office, take in the main sights, and have a meal. Then make your way back to the port area.

U Castille

This restaurant straddles both sides of the narrow cobbled alley leading to the famous Escalier du Roi d'Aragon. It has the advantage of being open much of the year, with a tiny outdoor terrace — a sun trap, even in late autumn. It's fun to sit here and watch tourists

> **U CASTILLE**
> Rue Simon Varsi, Haute Ville
> ℂ 04 95 73 04 99
> www.hotel-bonifacio-corse.fr
> closed Sundays and 15 Nov to 15 Mar €€ (menu at 25 €)
>
> **entrées** include the ubiquitous omelette with *brocciu*, fish soup *(soupe de poissons)*, *moules* or *aubergines à la Bonifacienne* (see overleaf), salad of warm goats' cheese, several pastas — including pasta with salmon or, more unusually, crayfish
>
> **fish and seafood** of all kinds — squid, swordfish, giant prawns, *pageot* (a sea bream), red mullet, sea bass, sole, crab, John Dory
>
> **meat** dishes: veal, lamb shanks, wild boar stew *(civet de sanglier)*, roast suckling pig *(porcelet rôti)*
>
> eight different **pizzas**

Our sea bass *(loup)* at U Castille was presented whole, then filleted for us and served with wild mushrooms. Delicious!

making their way up to the steps … and then back down again, having decided it's all too much effort. Or the cars roaring down the alley (little more than a foot-path), braking hard opposite the terrace, and picking up their U Castille take-away pizzas. The restaurant is part of the family-run Hotel Colomba, and the service is very friendly.

restaurants
eat

walk & eat CORSICA

This is *the* recipe for Corsican stuffed aubergines — 'à la Bonifacienne'. Frankly, Pat was a bit disappointed — not with the aubergines, but the *sauce,* which was so strong that it masked the taste of the other ingredients.

A few days later we asked Marie at Le Refuge (page 31) about it. (Marie was full of cooking tips.) She thought we might prefer the dish made 'à la mode de Porto-Vecchio': the tomato sauce *(without onion)* is simmered for only 5-10 minutes *(not 30min)* and so is less acidic. She also recommends using a *brocciu demi-sec*, not *sec* as in this main recipe. And Pat *does* prefer it Porto-Vecchio-style (as served at Le Refuge and shown at the right), but we give the *standard* recipe below, the one everyone else seems to love!

Stuffed aubergines, Bonifacio-style
(aubergines farcies à la Bonifacienne)

Preheat the oven to 180°C/350°F/gas mark 4. Meanwhile, first make the sauce by frying the garlic and onion in a little olive oil until glossy, then combine with the strained tomatoes in a saucepan (fresh tomatoes are used in restaurants, but who has the time!). Add the sugar, salt and pepper and simmer for 30min or more, until it is *very thick*. Set aside.

Cut the aubergines in half, lengthwise, and cook 5min in salted boiling water. Drain and remove the pulp *carefully,* so as not to cut to the skin. Put the pulp in a sieve and drain for 15min, then chop.

Soak the bread in the milk, then crumble it and put in a bowl. Add the 2 garlic cloves, grated cheese, chopped basil, pulp and beaten eggs. Season and mix well. Put the stuffing into a casserole and warm it in the oven for a few minutes, to dry it out, then stuff the aubergines with it.

recipes

eat

Heat about 75 ml of olive oil (5 tbsp) in heavy frying pan and fry the aubergines, *face down*, for 2min, until golden. (This takes some doing, so that the stuffing doesn't fall out — use a couple of long, wide spatulas.) Turn and do the skin side for another 2min.

Put the tomato sauce into a baking dish and place the aubergines on top. Bake for 15min. Spoon some of the sauce on top before serving.

Stuffed aubergines *Porto-Vecchio style*, at Le Refuge (see page 31)

Ingredients (for 4 people)
4 aubergines
2 eggs, beaten
150 g stale bread
150 ml milk
100 g *brocciu sec*, grated (or dry ricotta)
a few basil leaves, chopped
2 garlic cloves, crushed

for the sauce
400 g skinned fresh (or tinned plum) tomatoes, juice and seeds removed; strained
1 medium onion, chopped
1 garlic clove, minced
1 tsp sugar
olive oil
salt and pepper

No book with Corsican recipes would be complete without the next dish; it's on all the menus. While we needn't tell you how to make a cheese omelette, this one has a twist you might not expect: *you need 8 fresh mint leaves!*

Omelette with *brocciu* (not shown) (*omelette au brocciu*)

For four people, in addition to the mint you will need 300 g *brocciu frais* (or ricotta) and 8 eggs. Break the cheese into largish bits with a fork, and chop the mint. Beat the eggs with a fork and put the cheese and mint in *now*. Season and mix well. Then cook the mixture as you would a normal plain omelette.

This walk, one of the most beautiful in the south, is perfect for the whole family. Paths soft with pine needles and aglow with cyclamen in spring, take you to a grassy plateau with attractively eroded rocks *(tafoni)*, from where the *'sportifs'* can forge a way up to the cross on 'Dead Cow Peak'. A superb restaurant will reward your efforts!

forêt de l'ospédale

WALK 2

forêt de l'ospédale **walk 2**

Foce Alta

Start out just to the left of the parking bay: follow the clear **Sentier des Tafoni** (**❶**), where the Corsican Forestry Department has created a lovely woodland nature trail through the **Forêt de l'Ospédale**. Follow the copious *yellow flashes* and infrequent blue dots. Cross a **bridge** (**10min**) and five minutes later turn right on a crossing track. But after only 70m/yds, where the track makes a U-turn to the left, go sharp left on the **continuation of your path** (**❷**).*
Meeting a second track, turn right for just a few paces and **pick up the path again** (**❸**; almost opposite). Soon you join the orange flashes of the **Mare à Mare Sud**, a woodland trail coming from the right: follow it left (**35min**).

Distance: 4km/2.5mi; 1h15min

Grade: easy ascent of 100m/325ft on woodland paths; well waymarked, *but in heavy mist it's best to retrace the yellow-marked path from Foce Alta.* IGN map 4254 ET

Equipment: see page 12; no special equipment needed, except warm clothing in cool weather

Transport: 🚗 car to/from the Sentier des Tafoni nature trail: leave the D386 1km north of l'Ospédale, turning left for 'Agnaronu, Cartalavonu, Tavogna'. Referring to the 🚗→ symbols on the map, fork left (200m), left (400m), and left again (for 'Le Refuge, Cartalavonu'). Park 500m uphill, at the trail (sign: 'Sentier des Tafoni'. For 🚌 information, see page 132 under 'Walk 2'.

Refreshments:
Le Refuge at Cartalavonu (page 31)

Points of interest:
forestry nature trail
tafoni — rocks eroded into whimsical shapes
nearby Barrage de l'Ospédale

Watch out, 10 minutes along, for a narrow **path down to the left** (**❹**; there may be a blue dot on a tree) — your return route.

*This was the route when we last did the walk; if the waymarking has changed, follow the track to the Col de Mela and use the map from there.

walk & eat CORSICA

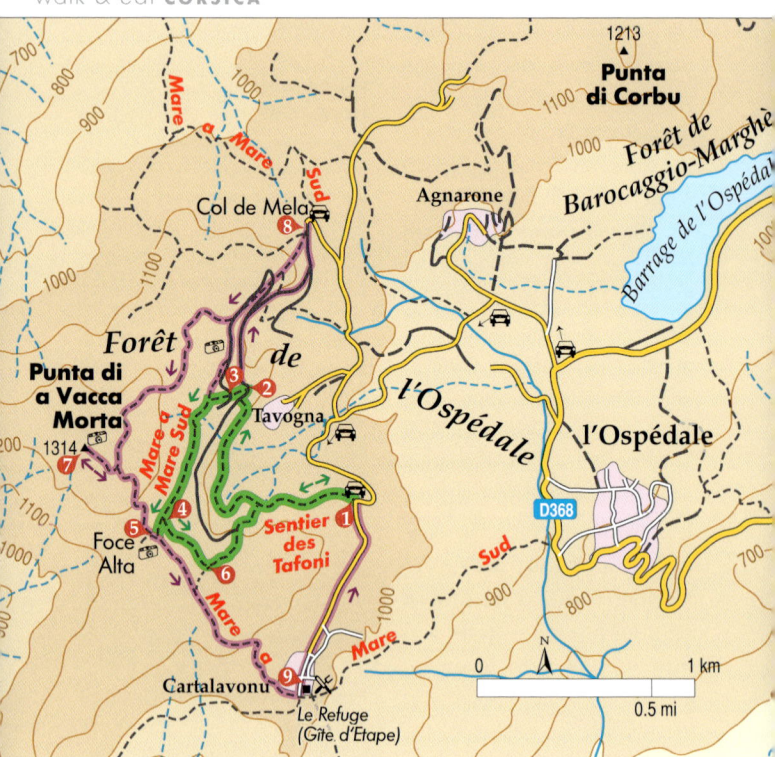

Two minutes later, **signposts** point the way right to the Vacca Morta (**7**), back the way you've come to the Col de Mela (**8**) and left down to Cartalavonu (**9**) — all possible variations of this walk shown on the map and for which GPS tracks are available. Head left a short way, to find a resting place here at **Foce Alta** (**5**; **47min**), among the *tafoni*, pines and tall grasses.

forêt de l'ospédale **walk 2**

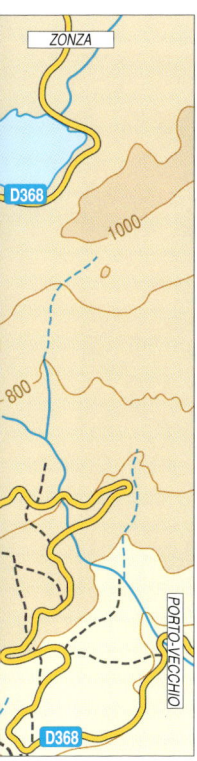

Sentier des Tafoni, just before Foce Alta; below: cyclamen brighten the path in spring.

Retrace your steps from the signposts for 120m/yds and turn right down the path (which may be marked by **sparse blue dots**). In seven minutes (about 350 metres), *be sure to turn left downhill* (**6**; **fluorescent waymarks** when last seen). Cross the end of a track and head half-right (**blue/yellow waymarks; post**). Quickly joining your outward path, turn right, back to the **Sentier des Tafoni** signpost (**1**; **1h15min**).

Barrage de l'Ospédale

Le Refuge

We first found this restaurant 32 years ago and could hardly believe our luck. It was tucked away in the woods — a popular *gîte d'étape* for walkers on the Mare à Mare Sud, but otherwise seemed only frequented by locals and some French tourists. Now

> **LE REFUGE**
> Forêt de l'Ospédale, Cartalavonu
> (04 95 70 00 39
> no website; on Facebook
> open 1 Apr-30 Oct; non-stop from 09.00-23.00; no credit cards €€-€€€
>
> **entrées** include traditional Corsican charcuterie, terrine of wild boar with onion chutney, carpaccio of lonzo
>
> **traditional main courses** — aubergines stuffed with *brocciu* and basil (photo page 25), roast suckling pig *(porcelet rôti)*, lamb ragout with chestnuts *(tianu)*, veal or wild boar sautéed in a sauce of Corsican wine and tomato, served with polenta *(petti morti)*, grilled pork chops or entrecôte
>
> **sweets** like *fiadone* (see page 123) with orange, fresh *brocciu* with a local *eau de vie*, crème brulée with a chestnut sauce — and of course a selection of Corsican cheeses with fig chutney
>
> good **wine list** — try the Costa Rossa Figari red

Le Refuge in late October

it's rated as one of the top restaurants in Porto-Vecchio, despite it being at least half an hour's drive from town.

The ambiance is very casual and rustic, but the food is brilliant — really high-class cooking of Corsican specialities. A lady called Marie founded the restaurant over 38 years ago; it's now run by her son — who uses her recipes and has introduced live guitar music on Tuesday and Friday evenings, with Corsican folk songs. He seems to have expanded the lovely terrace as well. Not that we've ever enjoyed the terrace; we seem always to visit on gloomy days out of season, when the homely, comfy atmosphere inside is a real tonic, especially if we've been walking in the rain.

The menu is limited, and the dishes are all à la carte. But the portion size won't disappoint hearty eaters — after all, many of the guests are hungry walkers staying at the *gîte*. Local produce — likes cheeses, meats, chutneys and wines — are on sale too.

Corsican fig chutney *(confiture de figues)*

Wash the figs in cold water, drain and dry. Pierce them liberally with a small skewer. Place in a heavy-bottomed casserole and add the sugar, being sure to cover all the fruit.

Split the vanilla pod in two and cut into pieces. Sprinkle over the fruit, then add about two glasses of water. Bring just to the boil, then take off the scum. Cook over a very low heat for about 3 hours, removing the scum from time to time.

Drain the figs and ladle them into sterilised jam jars, pour the syrup on top and let them cool.

<u>Ingredients (for about 4 jars)</u>
1.5 kg green figs
600 g caster sugar
1 vanilla pod

recipes

eat

Wild boar stew with ceps (civet de sanglier aux cèpes)

This dish seems no longer to be on the menu; pity! We concocted the recipe from Marie's *ingredients*; this is *not* her recipe. She used this sauce for both boar and Corsican veal.

Cut the meat into 2.5 cm cubes. Marinate overnight with the following 8 listed ingredients (from carrot to red wine). The next day, remove the meat from the marinade and set aside. Then strain all the vegetables from the marinade and reserve. In a saucepan, reduce the wine by half, skimming off impurities.

Preheat the oven to 160°C/325°F/gas mark 4. Dry the meat on paper towels, season, and brown all sides in olive oil in a heavy skillet. Transfer to a casserole. Swish the reserved vegetables around in the skillet until they are lightly caramelised, then transfer to the casserole.

Pour in the wine reduction, stock and tomatoes. Stir in the tomato paste. Make sure the meat is covered (add more wine if necessary!). At this stage we tend to add another teaspoon of Corsican herbs. Bring to a simmer, cover, and transfer to the oven.

When meat is almost cooked (2h or so), add the mushrooms and cook for another 20min, then remove from the oven. Strain all the liquid into a saucepan and reduce to the desired volume (generally by at least half). Pour the sauce over the meat and heat the lot gently until warmed through.

Ingredients (for 4 people)
- 1.2 kg wild boar (or venison, veal or hare)
- 1 carrot, peeled and diced
- 1 stalk celery, peeled and diced
- 1 onion, peeled and diced
- 5 cloves garlic
- 6 juniper berries, crushed
- 2 bay leaves, crushed
- 1 tsp Corsican herbs
- 500 ml red wine
- 500 ml stock
- 400 g fresh or 100 g dry ceps (porcini mushrooms)
- 1 tsp tomato purée
- 75 g tomatoes, peeled and diced
- olive oil for browning

The Massif of Bavella, with its towering pink walls and magnificent pine woods, has a magnetic, irresistible beauty. This walk to the edge of the southern massif is shady and undemanding — perfect for a warm day. But it's not lacking in drama — you can either admire the 'shell-hole' from a distance, or climb right up to it!

bavella: trou de la bombe

WALK

bavella: trou de la bombe **walk 3**

The Aiguilles (Needles) de Bavella

Start out at the **Auberge du Col de Bavella** (**❶**; 300m east downhill from the parking area at the col). Take the lane (later forestry track) opposite the *auberge,* marked with the red and white flashes of the **GR20** and signposted '**Paliri**'. There is a **fountain** at the right. From the outset you have a superb view that stretches to the sea, but it's the formidable wall of rocky pink crags bulging out of the landscape and blocking your way that holds your attention. From here the modest settlement of Bavella is concealed by pine woods.

Distance: 6km/3.7mi; 2h

Grade: fairly easy, with overall ascents of under 150m/500ft; agility is required on the approach to the Trou de la Bombe. *IGN map 4253 ET*

Equipment: see page 12; walking boots recommended, but not mandatory

Transport: 🚗 or 🚌 (see page 132) to/from the Auberge du Col (300m east of the Col de Bavella)

Refreshments:
Auberge du Col de Bavella (see page 39)

Points of interest:
Aiguilles de Bavella
rock formations, including the Trou de la Bombe

Some 600m/yds from the *auberge,* fork right uphill (**❷**; **10min**) on a path (where you may spot some faded red/orange waymarks). This rises gently through ferns and pines. Ten minutes uphill you pass a path off right (red/orange waymarks), signposted 'Bavella par la Chapelle' (**❸**; your **return route**). Go straight on here (red waymarks, signposted '**Pianona**', '**Compuleddu**'. Two minutes later, at a Y-fork, '**Compuleddu**' is signposted down to the left. Although that is our destination, first we'll make a short detour.

Fork *right uphill* here for '**Pianona**' (*not* waymarked). An

35

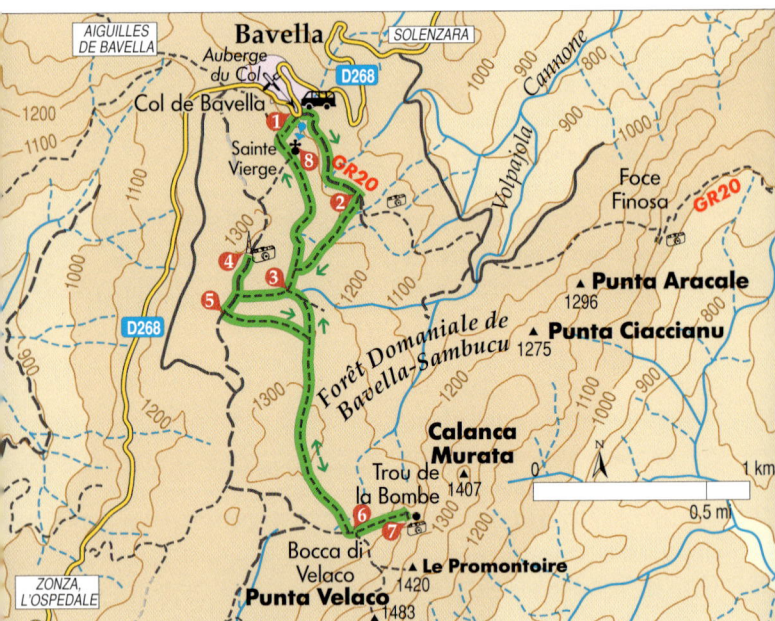

easy ascent of eight minutes brings you to a crossing track at the top of a rise, at the setting shown overleaf. The trees are too high here: walk just over 100m/yds to the right, to the **Pianona viewpoint** (**4**; **30min**) — a clearing by a telecoms mast, for a good view to the spiky Aiguilles (Needles) de Bavella.

Return past where you joined the track and, 300m further on, fork left on a **waymarked track** (**5**). This narrows to a path and brings you back to the main path in four minutes: turn right on this wider, crossing path. The gently undulating path bring you to a barrage of signposts at the **Bocca di Velaco** (**6**; **55min**).

bavella: trou de la bombe **walk 3**

Torou de la Bombe

The Bavella forest, on the way to the Pianona viewpoint

Cairned paths (*not* signposted) lead almost straight ahead from this pleasant clearing up to the jagged heights of Punta Velaco and le Promontoire. But we turn *left* here (red waymarks). After about seven minutes, take a path climbing up to the right (red waymarking on trees). In two minutes you're just below the 'shell-hole' (❼; **Trou de la Bombe**; **1h05min**). Red flashes show the best way to the hole itself, if you're very agile … and brave.

Back at the Bocca di Velaco, follow '**Bavella par la Chapelle**', retracing your outgoing route. Once back at the sign for the Pianona detour, go right; then, two minutes later, fork left (❸), now following waymarked paths to the **Chapelle de la Sainte Vierge** (❽; **1h50min**) and from there to **Bavella** (❶; **2h**).

Auberge du Col de Bavella

If you love mountains inns, then you'll love the Auberge du Col. But *do* work up an appetite before arriving; this *gîte d'étape* caters for walkers, and the portions of traditional, hearty Corsican fare are *huge*. There is a large airy dining room and a lovely terrace, but outside the main season, we prefer the more intimate snug (where they also sell Corsican goodies). Like Le Refuge on page 31, this inn is family-run (since 1936), and the younger generation have introduced guitar evenings with Corsican folk music.

AUBERGE DU COL
300m east of the Col de Bavella
(04 95 72 09 87
www.auberge-bavella.com
closed mid-Nov to mid-Mar, otherwise open daily, all day €€-€€€
menu at 29 €

for **entrées** there are salads, various pâtés, charcuterie, Bavella ham with melon

Corsican specialities: soup with ham bone, omelette with *brocciu*, aubergines or courgettes stuffed with *brocciu*, Corsican-style veal tripe, stew of haricot beans with *panzetta* (see page 130), wild boar stew with polenta, veal sauté with penne, Corsican veal cutlets with honey sauce, roast goat

all kinds of **pastas**

Corsican **cheeses** and sweets like chestnut or pear tart, apple cake

good **wine list**

restaurants
eat

Veal cutlets in honey sauce with mushrooms
(côtelettes de veau corse au miel)

First prepare the sauce: in a saucepan, reduce the stock to half. In another pan, cook the sugar and vinegar until the mixture caramelises.

Add the stock, honey, salt and pepper to taste, and cornflour. Bring to a boil, then set aside.

Fry the cutlets in olive oil (or grill if you prefer) and keep warm.

Sauté the mushrooms in butter, then add the honey sauce to the mushrooms and heat through. Pour over the cutlets and sprinkle with parsley.

Veal cutlet in honey sauce at the Auberge de Bavella, where the veal is cooked on a wood fire. Honey is a very popular ingredient on the island, and in all France only Corsican honeys carry an AOC designation. Some Corsican honeys are really strong. Since Corsican veal is more strongly flavoured than pen-reared meat, it might be better, back home, to use this sauce on pork cutlets.

Ingredients (for 4 people)
- 4 large veal or pork cutlets
- 2 garlic cloves, crushed
- 150 g buttom mushrooms
- 400 ml veal or chicken stock
- 50 g granulated sugar
- 50 ml red wine vinegar
- 2 tbsp chestnut (or strongly-flavoured) honey
- 1 tsp cornstarch, dissolved in water
- fresh parsley
- salt and pepper to taste
- olive oil and butter for frying

The *auberge* claims to be the only place on the island that makes this superb pie. We've tried to match the taste; the consistency is like a mince pie. In fact, why not try substituting 100 g mincemeat, to make a 'Christmas chestnut tart', flavouring it with brandy or rum in place of the vanilla.

Chestnut tart
(tarte aux châtaignes)

We've used gram (chick pea) flour for the base — a crispy pastry that doesn't need pre-baking. Use any base you like.

Mix the sugar with the flour and sift. Bring the flour/sugar and butter or margarine together with cold hands or in a food processor. When it has the consistency of breadcrumbs, mix in the water and lightly knead into a ball. Wrap in cling film and set aside for 30min.

Meanwhile, preheat the oven to 180°C/325°F/gas mark 4 and grease a 20 cm/8 in circular loose-bottomed tin.

Stir together the chestnuts, sugar, honey and vanilla. Add the eggs and mix well.

Roll out the pastry, line the tin, bottom and sides, and pour in the filling. Bake for about 30-40min, until a toothpick inserted into the centre comes out clean. Sprinkle with powdered sugar to serve. Good warm or cold — with cream or ice cream.

Ingredients
(for 10 servings)

for the base:
100 g gram flour
1 tbsp caster sugar
50 g butter or hard margarine
1-2 tbsp cold water

for the filling:
400 g prepared chestnuts, roughly chopped
3 tbsp caster sugar
2 large eggs, beaten
1 tsp vanilla
3 tbsp chestnut honey

to serve:
icing sugar

This easy out-and-back (or alternative, circular) walk puts you into the holiday mood straight away. It gives you a taste of the beaches to come, and takes you through picturesque countryside. In spring you'll be intoxicated by the sweet-smelling *maquis,* when the hillsides are ablaze with a riot of brightly-coloured flowers.

pointe de la parata
WALK

The walk begins at the **Visitors' Centre** at the **Pointe de la Parata** (❶). This rocky promontory is the site of a 17th-century Genoese tower, built as a defence against the Moors. Beyond the point lie the Iles Sanguinaires, a group of sharp granite islets. Join the crowds (this walk has become massively popular in the last few years) and take the road on the east side of the peninsula out to the restaurant/souvenir shop (**15min**). If you want a *very* easy walk — just a stroll — walk from here round the tower, or climb up to it. If you are going to round the tower *in addition* to the main walk, add about half an hour to the walk timings.

Now take the **gravelly path** (❷) at the left-hand side of the restaurant. Immediately you're swallowed up in *maquis*. In spring an array of flowers holds your attention all along, and yellow spiny broom lights up the hillsides. You head round into an aquamarine-coloured bay, set at the foot of dark green hills.

Distance: up to 13.5km/8.4mi; 3h05min (the walk can be shortened at any point)

Grade: easy, but some thorny scrub on route. No shade on beaches, can be very hot. Overall ascents/descents of 150m/490ft. *IGN map 4153 OT*

Equipment: as page 12; light shoes, sun protection, bathing things and plenty of water recommended

Transport: 🚗 or 🚌 (see page 132) to/from the Pointe de la Parata

Refreshments: restaurants at the Pointe de la Parata and along the D111 (see Alternative walk)

Alternative walk: Pointe de la Parata — Sevani — D111 (11km/6.8mi; 2h45min; grade as main walk, but with overall ascents and descents of 280m/920ft). Access by bus as above. Follow the main walk to Sevani, climb the lane up to the D111b, and turn right downhill to the D111 (bus shelter and restaurant — see page 46).

Points of interest: seascapes, coastal flora, Genoese tower

Rising past a maze of paths coming from the car park, you will see your ongoing route ahead: a dirt track following the west coast (**25min**). It's locally called the 'Customs Officers' Trail' — the **Sentier des Douaniers**. Make your way over to it, maybe in the company of the odd car bumping along to one of the flower-filled weekend retreats. After crossing a low crest above the **Pointe de la Corba** (❸; **45min**), you look down into a small rocky cove. The track descends to it, but you bear right, keeping along the wide path. Lizards galore dart across your path, as you brush your way through flowers.

As you cross over a ridge (**1h15min**), a superb view greets you: two beautiful beaches rest in the now-flat coastline — the first small and circular, the second large and sweeping. An open grassy valley, sheltered by high rocky hills, empties out into the bay. The arm of the cape rolls out to the left. Descend to a track above the first cove, by the holiday hamlet of **Sevani** and its beach, the **Plage de St-Antoine** (or de Sevani; ❹; **1h27min**). From here head inland, if you're doing the Alternative walk.

To continue along the coast, squeeze through the rocks at the end of this blinding-white cove, and carry on up the bank. Just beyond the next cove, a clearer path leads you to the **Anse de Minaccia** (❺; **1h40min**) in unspoilt countryside. It's possible to continue along the coast for another hour or more, to take in more inviting, usually deserted coves. But we end here: return the same way to the **Pointe de la Parata** (❶; **3h05min**) — or take the inland route via the lane from Sevani, to emerge on the D111. A bus shelter is 100m to the right (❻); another is 300m to the left, above Le Weekend — our recommended restaurant.

Le Weekend

This restaurant is almost opposite the D111b where the Alternative walk emerges — it's just a little to the east, on the sea side of the road. It's been run by the same family since 1953; they have recently added a boutique hotel.

While the à la carte dishes and the wines are admittedly expensive (there is no *menu*), one *can* have a reasonably priced light meal — like the courgette fritters shown opposite or the goat cheese salad with all the trimmings. So treat yourself: the elegant white dining room or terrace, with views to the Iles Sanguinaires and the Pointe de la Parata, are delightful and very relaxing — and no one looked askance at our walkers' garb.

LE WEEKEND
at the km 7 marker on the D111
(Route des Iles Sanguinaires)
(04 95 52 01 39
www.hotel-le-weekend.com
lunch (from 12.00) and dinner (from 20.00), daily, Mar till Nov €€-€€€

entrées feature 6 different cold plates, including a tempura prawn salad and duck pâté; there are 3 hot entrées — stuffed clams, fish soup, and *beignets* with a *coulis* of tomatoes (see opposite)

mains include 5-6 kinds of fresh **fish** — grilled or poached: cod, sea bass, daurade, various species of sea bream, rascasse, etc; also **seafood**: lobster *(very expensive!)*, crawfish, crayfish, giant prawns; **meats**: duck breast with pepper sauce or fillet of beef cooked over a wood fire with foie gras and a sauce of wine and beef marrow

Grilled darne of cod, fish of the day at Le Weekend, served with gooseberries in a white wine sauce

restaurants

eat

Courgette fritters
(beignets de courgettes)

First prepare the batter: in a bowl mix the flour, 1 tbsp of oil, 200 ml warm water, the egg yolk and a pinch of salt. The batter should be elastic but not too runny. Cover and set aside for 2 hours.

Make our quick 'cheat's' sauce: sweat the garlic and shallot in the oil, add the other ingredients and simmer for about 20-30min. It should be very thick and fairly sweet, *not* acidic. Remove the bouquet garni, toss in some more fresh parsley and mint if you like, and set aside to cool. (Some recipes add sliced olives and fresh anchovies.)

Wash and clean the courgettes, but do not peel. Slice them about 7 mm (1/4 in) thick and place in a wide, deep dish. Add 2 tsp of oil, the lemon juice, parsley, mint, salt and pepper. Mix and let marinate for an hour, then remove.

Beat the egg white into stiff peaks and fold into the batter. Heat the oil to 175°C/350°F. Mix the courgettes in the batter and fry until golden and puffed up. Drain on paper towels and serve at once, very hot.

Ingredients (for 4 people)

for the fritters
5 smallish thin-skinned courgettes
200 g flour
500 ml sunflower or similar oil
1 egg, separated
juice of 1 lemon
4 sprigs flat parsley, minced
4 fresh mint leaves, minced
salt and ground pepper

for the sauce (coulis)
400 g tinned tomatoes
20 ml olive oil
2 garlic cloves, crushed
1 shallot, minced
2 tsp sugar
1 tsp tomato concentrate
1 bouquet garni

recipes
eat

The cascading Agnone River is the essence of this walk, bounding downstream below Corsica's fifth-highest peak. An apron of pines covers Monte d'Oro's lower slopes, but the valley is home to a splendid beech forest. Of all these beautiful gifts of nature, it's the river you'll remember … and the dazzling Cascades des Anglais.

cascades des anglais
WALK

cascades des anglais **walk 5**

The walk begins at the car park at the **Col de Vizzavona** (❶). Walk uphill following the sign for the Cascades des Anglais (yellow flashes). Monte d'Oro (2389m/7835ft) soon appears through the beech trees, filling in this picture. Its naked rocky crown rises high above the pine wood patching its inclines.

You rise quickly to ruined **Fort Vaux** (❷) shown on page 51. Keep the fort to your left and follow the good yellow-waymarked path east along the ridge. When the path meets a track coming from the adventure park on the T20, turn left (❸; **15min**). Then the track makes a U-bend down to the right; here keep straight ahead on a **path** (❹) — to the crystal-clear, bubbly river, with its green and alluring pools. The GR20 from Vizzavona crosses the **bridge** here (❺; **30min**); there is a seasonal

On the GR20 near Vizzavona's railway station

Distance: 3.1km/1.9mi; 1h05min

Grade: moderate, but you must be sure-footed; descent/ascent of about 170m/560ft. *IGN map 4251 OT*

Equipment: see page 12; walking boots recommended — or stout shoes; bathing things in hot weather

Transport: 🚗 to/from the Col de Vizzavona on the T20, where there is a large free car park (42° 6.730'N, 9° 6.759'E). Or 🚂 to/from Vizzavona (see page 132): from the Vizzavona railway station (❶ₐ) take the road uphill to the right (signposted to the GR20, the Cascades des Anglais, and the Pin Laricio Nature Trail). *Carefully follow the red/white GR waymarks and signposts to the bridge over the Agnone, cross it, and pick up the main walk at its 30min-point, at ❺ (adding 45min to all times).*

Refreshments:
Hotel du Monte d'Oro (see page 56)

Alternative walk: Old CAF refuge (8.5km/5.3mi; 3h50min in total, but add 30min each way if travelling by train). See notes on page 52. A wonderful hike for the energetic; see pages 52-53.

Points of interest:
Agnone river, local history

49

walk & eat **CORSICA**

Cascades des Anglais

kiosk as well), while the nature trail keeps to the north side of the river.

Remaining on the south side of the river, we now follow the GR. There is no single clearly-trodden path, so follow the red and white waymarks carefully. The Agnone bounces down the valley alongside you, one falls after another — the **Cascades des Anglais** (❻). At the top of the last cascade, a large **cairn** (❼); **45min**) on the left alerts you to your route back to the car park. *(If you first want to press ahead up the valley, see overleaf.)*

Turn left and head back southeast above the GR, contouring through a cairned rock chaos and then beech woods. After 15 minutes, at a Y-fork, turn right, up to the top of the ridge and back to

The remains of the old Fort Vaux on the ridge above the Col de Vizzavona; its stones were used to rebuild the Chapel of Our Lady of the Snows (see page 55).

the ruins of Fort Vaux (❷), which you reach in just a couple of minutes. Keeping the ruin on your left, retrace your steps to the car park at the **Col de Vizzavona** (❶; **1h05min**).

Alternative walk to the old CAF refuge: Continue ahead at the 45min-point (**5**), still on the GR20. The route is very steep at times; sometimes you'll be using all fours. Green lichen illuminates the surrounding rock; under direct sunlight it glows with the fluorescence of a highlighter pen. Ignore a turn-off to the left at the **Bergeries de Porteto** (**8**), then cross the river on a **footbridge** (**1h55min**), above a small but thundering waterfall. Continue as far as you like — perhaps to the scant remains of the old French Alpine Club (CAF) **refuge** (**9**; **2h15min**), where the spring snow-line is not far out of reach. Just below this small crumbled shelter is the largest waterfall in the valley. You're

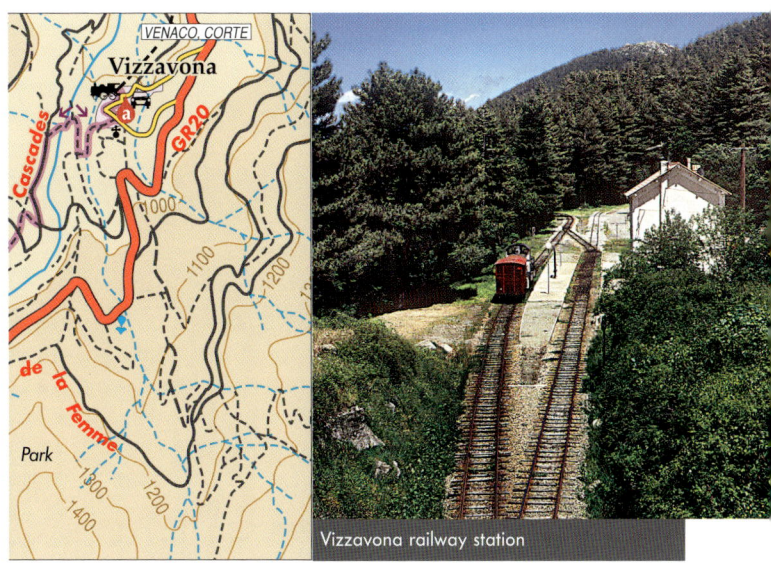

Vizzavona railway station

completely encircled by mountains. In the hills to the south, the Monte Renoso chain may still be wearing a mantle of snow.

Heading back, don't miss the beryl-green pools that lie concealed in the valley floor; some are magnificent. But if you decide to swim, make sure they're safe; the current can be very strong. You will be back at the top end of the **cascades** in about 1h25min (**7**); **3h40min**). Watch for the large cairn alerting you to your return path (described on page 51) and retrace your steps to the **Col de Vizzavona** (**1**; **3h50min**). Or cross the bridge and follow the GR/nature trail back to **Vizzavona station** (**a**) — for an overall time of about **4h35min**, excluding stops.

Hôtel du Monte d'Oro

This hotel, run by the same family for just over 100 years, was originally built to house engineers piercing the 4km-long tunnel for the railway (see page 125). It became a hotel in 1880 and was

The dining room at the Hôtel du Monte d'Oro — unchanged since the 1880s

bought by the present owners in 1904 (the *refuge* on the main road also belongs to them). The first visitors were wealthy people from Bastia, Ajaccio, Paris … and England — who saw it as a low-key hill station from where they could enjoy pleasant shaded walks — hence the name 'Waterfalls of the English'.

The place is just wonderful — a step back in time to a more

leisurely era. The dining room — like a garden, full of plants — is still as it was at end of 19th century, with turned wood chairs, thick white napkins and silver cutlery. You will enjoy fine, traditional Corsican cooking. If you're enjoying a coffee in the lounge afterwards, ask to see the book of the hotel's history; the notes are in English as well as French.

Our Lady of the Snows

One of the stories concerns the chapel of Our Lady of the Snows in the hotel grounds (where Sunday services are still held). During World War Two the original, wooden chapel was used by occupying Italian troops to house their mules. When the chaplain of the Italian Army came to the hotel, Mme Plaisant showed him how it had been desecrated.

He evicted the animals, burned the chapel down (to purify it), and had the Army rebuild it in stone. The stone came from the 17th-century Fort Vaux in the photo on page 53. In fact there was a 16th-century pilgrimage chapel up by the fort, dedicated to St Peter. So, as the history poignantly says, 'the stones returned to their original religious significance'.

In 1940 Ajaccio's military hospital was moved to the hotel. After the war, German prisoners helped to rebuild the hotel and later came back to visit the owners and introduce their families.

HÔTEL DU MONTE D'ORO
Col de Vizzavona
(04 95 47 21 06
www.monte-oro.com
open from 1 May to early Oct €€

trout (locally caught) is a speciality — bleu, meunière, with pine nuts (see page 57)

Corsican **soup**, **omelettes, salads, charcuterie** for a lighter meal

meats include steaks, pork, veal, duck in honey sauce (see page 56)

good selection of **sweets** and **wines** (especially from around Ajaccio)

The hotel uses its own citrus- and *maquis*-flavoured honey for this dish; it's a pity they only produce enough for their own needs!

Duck breast with honey sauce *(magret de canard au miel)*

Fry the mushrooms gently in butter for 15min, turning once or twice. Set aside and keep warm. Cook the duck in a separate, heavy skillet, having first pricked the skin to avoid bursting: fry skin side down at a very high heat for 6min, then turn and fry more gently for another 4min with the crushed garlic cloves. Season, remove from pan and keep warm. (After 10min, slice quite thinly and pour the juices back into the skillet.)

Ingredients (for 4 people)
- 4 duck breasts, preferably French
- 4 tbsp clear aromatic honey
- 150 ml duck or chicken stock
- 2 tbsp raspberry vinegar
- 1 box 'fruits of the forest'
- 400 g fresh ceps (porcini mushrooms)
- 2 cloves garlic, crushed
- 1 tsp tomato paste
- 75 g tomatoes, peeled and diced
- salt, freshly-ground pepper
- 2 tbsp butter, in small pieces

Put half the fruits, the tomatoes, tomato paste and garlic in a saucepan with the stock and boil rapidly to reduce to half. Put this reduction into the skillet and bring to a simmer. Add the honey and let it caramelise slightly. Then stir in the vinegar, strain and re-season. Add the rest of the fruit and heat through. Add the butter bit by bit, whisking to a fairly thick, glossy sauce. Sweat the mushrooms separately and stir them in just before serving.

recipes
eat

Trout with pine nuts *(truites aux pignons)*

Preheat the oven to 190°C/375°F/gas mark 5. Season the trout and place, whole, in an ovenproof dish with the onion, herbs, lemon slice and wine. Cover with foil and bake for about 20min, until tender.

Remove the trout from the baking dish; set aside and keep warm. (You may prefer at this stage to fillet the fish; at the Hôtel Monte d'Oro it is served whole.) Strain the cooking liquid; you should be left with 150 ml — add some water or fish stock if short.

Melt the butter in a saucepan over a low heat, sprinkle in the flour bit by bit and, stirring vigorously, cook to a paste. Slowly add the cooking liquid, stirring constantly to avoid lumps, and bring to the boil. Add the cream (still stirring), and bring to the boil again. Reduce the heat, stir in the pine nuts and warm through. Season.

Pour the sauce over the fish and sprinkle with parsley. We think it's best served with *fluffy* rice, as here. Lately it's fashionable on Corsica to serve a rice 'timbale' (moulded, as in the photograph with the duck opposite), taken more recently.

Ingredients (for 4 people)

4 trout, about 200 g each
200 m dry white wine
1 small onion, minced
1 bay leaf, some fresh thyme, parsley and a slice of lemon
25 g butter
1 tbsp flour
150 ml single cream
150 g pine nuts
salt and freshly-ground black pepper
chopped parsley to garnish

This tour of the three Venacos is a lovely complement to a journey on the little train. For the energetic, the whole 'Venachese' area, at the heart of the Parc Natural Régional, is a walking centre *par excellence*, a crossroads of the long-distance Mare à Mare Nord and many shorter, locally-marked routes (Sentiers du Pays).

the venacos

WALK

the venacos **walk 6**

Santo-Pietro-di-Venaco

Start out at **Poggio-Riventosa station** (**1**): follow the D140 uphill into **Poggio-di-Venaco** (**25min**). *Pass* the small electricity transformer building on the left and take the next left turn (the cypress-framed **war memorial** will be behind you). You are on a variant of the Mare à Mare Nord, *sparsely* marked with orange flashes, but there should be a walker' signpost here: '**Corte, Casanova**').

In two minutes, as you pass below a **cemetery** on the left, go right down steps (cairns, arrow), to cut a bend off the road. Then, when the road makes a U-bend to the right, go left downhill on path in deep shade (arrow; cairn). You cross a burbling stream on a **footbridge**. After rising through a ferny dell, on the approach to Casanova, veer right to a tarred lane and follow it at the left of a stone

Distance: 9.7km/6mi; 3h50min

Grade: moderate, with ascents/descents of about 400m/1300ft overall. *IGN map 4251 OT*

Equipment: as page 12; walking boots recommended

Transport: 🚆 to Poggio-Riventosa *(request stop!)*; return from Venaco (see page 133). Or 🚗 to Venaco station and take the train to Poggio-Riventosa to start the walk.

Shorter circuit: quite easy; 6km/3.7mi; 2h15min; 🚗 or 🚆. Follow the main walk (omitting the detour into Riventosa) to Santo-Pietro. Have lunch, then return to Riventosa. Walk up past the church and the fine view towards Corte (**4**), then curl down to the D40. Turn left and, almost at once, at the end of the wall, fork right on a footpath. This soon meets D149: follow it to your car at Poggio or walk on to the railway station (**1**).

Refreshments en route:
Restaurants in Poggio-di-Venaco and Casanova
Le Torrent and Le Petit Bosquet in Santo-Pietro (see page 64)
Bar/Restaurant de la Placein Venaco (see page 65)

Points of interest:
high-mountain surroundings at the centre of the Regional Natural Park

59

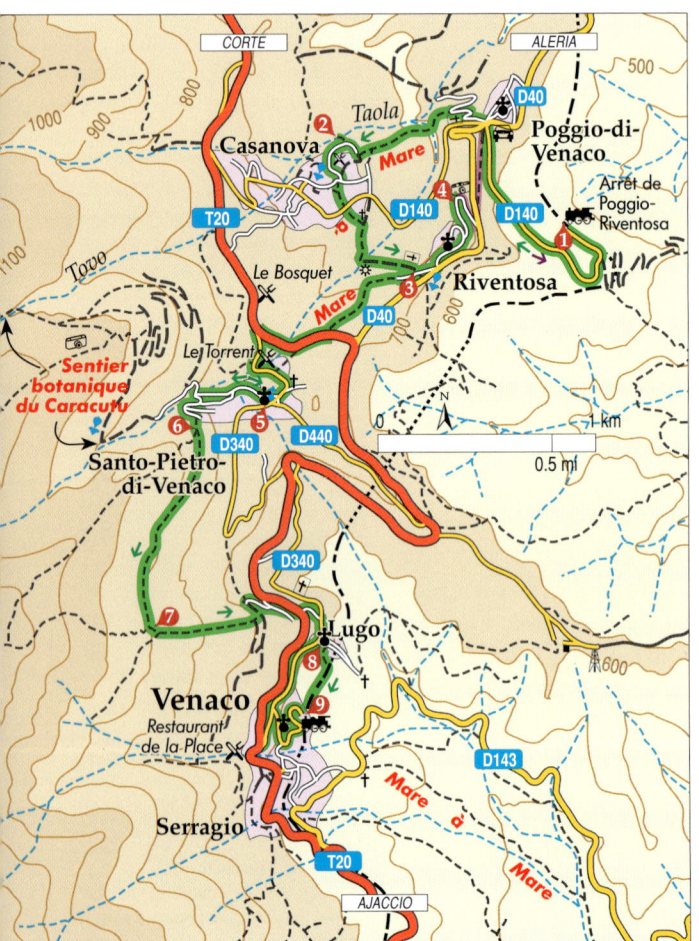

Top: detail on a tomb in Poggio-di-Venaco; below: the Ruisseau de Taola

hut with a house behind. You will later follow the road uphill to the left, but first walk down either path to the pretty **Ruisseau de Taola** (❷; **40min**).

The road rises past a restaurant on the left to a **fountain** and benches on the right, where you are likely to see the some splashes of orange paint. You now skirt **Casanova**, where there are some traditional slate-roofed buildings on the left. You come to a T-junction with another road; go straight over the crossing road onto a cobbled path (walkers' sign: '**Riventosa, San Petru**'). Rise up to the D140 and cross it (**50min**). Ignore a track to the left (by a **tomb** with cypresses) and keep ahead towards Riventosa, spread out along a ridge above to the left. The path contours at the left of a drystone wall, then crosses another tinkling stream on a **footbridge** (**55min**) and passes the **Moulin de Riventosa** on the right (information board).

Soon a shady track takes you up

Churches of Poggio-di-Venaco (left) and Santo-Pietro-di-Venaco

to **Riventosa**. Walk to the right of the **cemetery**, then curl up right on tar. Pass a lane off right signed to 'San Petru' (❸; **1h05min**; you will return to this to continue the walk). Joining the main D40 a minute later (**tap**, **war memorial**), turn left up the cobbled road through the village centre, past the **church** on the left. At a Y-fork, go right up a narrow road, to a tremendous **viewpoint** (❹) towards Corte.

Then return to the 1h05min-point in the walk (❸; the lane signposted to 'San Petru'). Follow the orange waymarks of the Mare à Mare to the **T20** (**1h45min**). Turn right, pass the Le Bosquet on the right (a possible lunch venue if Le Torrent is not open), then walk to the junction with the narrow D340. Turn sharp left here, to pass the old **Château Pozzo di Borgo** on the left. (The château, shown overleaf, houses the hotel Le Torrent, our recommended restaurant — although we've not been there since it changed hands.)

Continue the gentle ascent on the D340, past a **war memorial** on the left, and keep right to come to the lovely **church** (**❺**) at **Santo-Pietro-di-Venaco**. From here the easiest option is just to follow the Mare à Mare to Venaco, but it is mostly along the same narrow road. Our suggested way on to Venaco takes a somewhat higher route: walk up the road at the right of the church. At a T-junction by a **bridge**, go left, then turn right to the top of the village, the highest point of the walk (**3h**). Climb the signposted path on the right to a **Y-fork** (**❻**), where arrows point in both directions: take the path to the left here. This path, an orange waymarked 'Sentier de Pays' (local walk) rises 100m/300ft and contours at about 900m, to a **crossroads of paths** (**❼**). Go left now, down to the **T20** (**3h20min**).

Cross the road and follow the road almost opposite (slightly to the right) down into **Lugo**, crossing the D340.

If you don't want to visit Venaco, you can take a short-cut to the railway station: fork right on a stone-laid path behind Lugo's **church** (**❽**), down to the railway *line.* Walk along the track to the right for 150m, to **Venaco station** (**❾**; **3h35min**).

If you *do* want to visit Venaco, from Lugo's church follow the D340 south to a Y-fork (just before Venaco's **church**). Go right, uphill, here (the road to the left leads down to the station). The Restaurant de la Place is on the far side of the T20 in the centre of **Venaco**, just to the left. From there descend the same way, to walk back to the **railway station** (**❾**; **3h50min**).

Le Torrent

The IGN map shows a château at Poggio, locating it due east of the church. Expecting to see a tower or at least a turret or two, we just assumed it was in ruins when it never materialised over the years. But lunching at Le Torrent years ago, we realised we had found it: the hotel building dates from the late 19th century.

When we first found it an enthusiastic small new management team had just taken over, and while we dined off Limoges porcelain (!), they fretted over the décor. But when we checked in 2024

Le Torrent, once the château of the Pozzo di Borgo family

LE TORRENT
D340, Santo-Pietro-di-Venaco (also an entrance drive off the T20)
(04 20 13 06 95; letorrent.com
daily, all year €€

entrées, including tart with Corsican herbs, *escargots*, *moules*, local pâté, headcheese with a nut or raspberry vinegar

fresh **pastas**, including sauces with giant prawns or *brocciu*

brocciu **omelette**

fish: sea bass grilled with fennel or ginger, daurade in white wine or ginger and curry sauce, giant prawns cooked three different ways, trout — grilled or baked and stuffed with *brocciu*

meats: entrecôte, veal chop with sage and lemon, roast milk-fed lamb with Corsican herbs, slivers of chicken — either with ginger and honey, curry and coconut milk, mustard sauce, or lemon and vanilla

small **wine list**

restaurants
eat

the hotel was closed. Web searches imply that it has changed hands at least twice since our first visit, and reviews *for the hotel* differ wildly. Where the restaurant is mentioned in a review, the food is often praised — as is the shady outdoor eating area. Since we were unable to have lunch there during our last visit, we've left the menu and recipes as they were in the first edition of this book, because the few photos with web reviews suggest they still do similar dishes.

Bar/Restaurant de la Place

Totally different from the elegant Torrent, this is a relaxed, inexpensive meeting place on the main square in Venaco, where you can join the locals on the front terrace and watch lorries laden with huge

> **BAR/RESTAURANT DE LA PLACE**
> T20, Venaco centre ☏ 04 95 47 01 30
> facebook.com/barrestaurant.delaplace.9
> closed Nov €€
>
> **'menu corse'** at 30 €: three courses with a choice of Corsican charcuterie, Corsican salad or quiche Venaco-style (Venaco is well known for its ewes' milk cheese), followed by cannelloni with brocciu, veal stew with olives, or pork cutlets with ceps; Corsican cheeses or dessert of the day
>
> the à la carte menu lists various **entrées**: 6 **salads**, 10 **pizzas**, **omelettes**; **mains** include entrecôte, lamb chops, slivers of chicken, or chicken with curry; there are also various **tapas** (like courgette fritters) and **pastas** (like tagliatelli carbonara)

laricio pines trying to negotiate the U-bend.

Very friendly atmosphere; super-fresh local produce; excellent pizzas (and pizza take-aways).

Chicken in curry and coconut milk
(poulet au curry et au lait de coco)

First make the curry: heat the coriander and cumin seeds and the cardamom pods to dry them (either under a hot grill, or in a dry skillet, turning constantly for 1min), then mix with the ginger, fresh coriander and garlic. Crush all together until you have a paste, then add the fish sauce. Stir; set aside.

Heat the oil in a wok or large frying pan. Fry the chicken just to seal, then put in the onions and fry for another 2-3min. Add the curry paste and stock; mix well and simmer, covered, for 20min.

Pour in the coconut milk; add a few drops of lemon juice. Stir, then bring to the boil for a few minutes. Turn down the heat and simmer for another 10min, uncovered, to reduce.

Meanwhile, gently fry the spinach in oil for a few minutes. Serve the curry on a bed of basmati rice, decorated with the spinach leaves.

<u>Ingredients (for 4 people):</u>
- 4 chicken breast fillets, cut into thin strips
- 2 medium onions, minced
- small bag of spinach
- 500 ml chicken stock
- 200 ml coconut milk
- few drops lemon juice
- sesame or peanut oil for frying
- salt and pepper

for the curry paste:
- 1 tsp coriander seeds
- 2 cardamom pods, crushed
- 1 tsp ground ginger
- 2 tbsp fresh chopped coriander
- 1/2 tsp cumin seeds
- 2 garlic cloves, minced
- 2 tbsp Thai fish sauce

recipes
eat

We didn't have the chicken in curry at Le Torrent, but concocted a similar dish later at home which was quite easy to prepare (see opposite).

What we *did* have was leg of lamb in a lovely sauce. To prepare this lamb, stud it with garlic slivers as you would normally, but instead of adding rosemary, first lightly coat the lamb with oil, then roll it in Corsican herbs *(aromates du maquis)*. The lamb should be *completely* covered in the herbs. Roast as normal, then, when it is resting, scrape off some of the roasted herbs, ease out the garlic, and add to the pan juices with some white wine. After slicing the meat, add those juices as well and boil rapidly for a few minutes to reduce a bit.

Along with the lamb they served a *cake:* we didn't know what to expect, but this turned out to be a delicious vegetable 'custard' flavoured with cumin. We've tried to duplicate it below.

Vegetable 'cake' *(cake aux legumes)*, not illustrated

Preheat the oven to 180°C/350°F/gas mark 4. Grease 4 200 ml custard cups. Steam the leek, carrots and onion until tender (about 10min).

Beat the eggs and whisk in the cream and butter until smooth. Stir in the cumin and the cooked vegetables. Season.

Divide into the custard cups and bake in a bain-marie in the lower part of the oven for 40min, or until a knife inserted into the centre comes out clean. Run the knife round the edge of the cups to remove — *carefully!*

<u>Ingredients (for 4 people):</u>
1 leek, sliced
2 carrots, finely sliced
1 medium onion, diced
2 large eggs
2 tbsp heavy cream
2 tbsp unsalted butter, in small pieces
1 tsp cumin seeds
salt and pepper

If you've ever driven up the Restonica road with your heart set on walking to the Melo and Capitello lakes, then your heart will probably sink as you near the Pont de Grotelle! 'Flocks' of walkers — like so many sheep — clog the road, all intent on doing one of the island's best-known hikes.

la restonica WALK

la restonica walk 7

Monte Leonardo, by the Pont de Frasseta

Admittedly, the 'lakes' walk is a *must*. But for those of you who don't like crowds, or who want an easier option, this walk in a grandiose setting is a fine alternative, with many places to relax by the river or throw yourself into one of its emerald-green pools. And our recommended restaurant is just as brilliant as the hike!

Logistics are a problem. The ideal way to do the walk, *easily,* is to just descend from the Pont de Grotelle to the Pont de Frasseta, then continue 8km down the beautiful riverside *road* to the Auberge de la Restonica. Unless you're with friends, you will need a taxi from Corte. (Note that there is also an hotel at the *auberge.*) Otherwise, take a car or the minibus to do an out-and-back walk from Frasseta Bridge.

Distance: 9.5km/6mi; 4h *return*. If you are travelling with friends or a taxi, you can make this a one-way walk down from the Pont de Grotelle (1h45min).

Grade: moderate; descent/reascent of 350m/1150ft. You must be sure-footed (a few rock-falls to cross). Can be very cold; don't attempt in unpredictable weather. *IGN map 4251 OT*

Equipment: as page 12; walking boots, warm clothing or bathing things recommended, depending on the season

Transport: 🚗 to/from the Pont de Grotelle on the Restonica road (D623, 15km from Corte). Or, if you prefer to walk *uphill* first, park at the Pont de Frasseta (42° 15.681'N, 9° 4.343'E) or take a Line C13 🚌 to/from the Pont de Frasseta (frequent; see page 133)

Refreshments:
Auberge de la Restonica (see page 73), 2km up from Corte, 8km below the Pont de Frasseta; *none en route*

Points of interest:
Restonica River and surroundings university town of Corte

We **start out** at the **Pont de Grotelle** (❶), in the magical alpine setting shown on page 71. Cross the bridge, then turn right on a path (signpost: '**Pont de Frasseta 1h50min**'). Ample orange flashes, and some cairns, mark the route all the way to your destination — another bridge a little under 5km downstream. Majestic old pines shade the way and frame your photographs up to the peaks and down to the rushing **Restonica River**. The path undulates for most of the way, sometimes crossing fairly steep rock-falls (where cairns indicate the route if the orange-painted rocks have slipped away). After bumbling over a side-stream on 'stepping-stone' *boulders,* with a **waterfall** up to left (**35min**), before long the path is just beside the **river (50min)** — a fine place to swim, if you have time.

When you come to a wide **crossing path (1h)**, follow it to the left, eventually rising to a tiny grassy **plateau (1h10min)**. From here the path runs steeply downhill, crosses two adjacent streams, and then continues through ferns bright with foxgloves in spring. On the final short ascent, you look

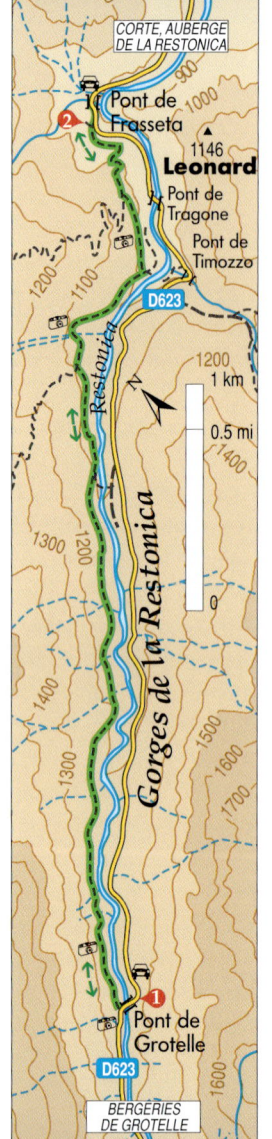

la restonica **walk 7**

Pont de Grotelle, at the start of the walk

The bounding Restonica River

straight out at **Monte Leonardo**, the rocky pinnacle shown on page 68. At the top of the climb (**1h30min**), just opposite this monolith, you come to a sign: '**Pont de Grotelle 2h**', pointing back the way you've come. Turn right at this path junction. Follow the gentle zigzags of the path down to the **Pont de Frasseta** parking area (**❷**; **1h45min**). From here it's a two hour stroll down the road to the Auberge de la Restonica, but *mind any traffic!* From the *auberge* it's a short 2km hop to Corte, for the train.

Or first return the same way to the **Ponte de Grotelle** (**❶**), if you left your car there (allow 2h15min, or **4h** in all).

Auberge de la Restonica

Don't miss this restaurant run by the same family for four generations! We took the picture at about 12.30; half an hour later the place was full of couples

or business people from Corte. The food was fabulous, one of the best meals we've had on the island. We couldn't manage the parfait, but sampled the chestnut brandy, both sweet *(doux)* and dry *(sec)*; both should be served cold. And the glorious setting, beside the river, is enchanting. *Next time,* we'll spend a night or two at the adjacent Hotel Dominique Colonna!

> **AUBERGE DE LA RESTONICA**
> Restonica road (D623), 2km up from Corte
> (04 95 46 09 58
> www.aubergerestonica.com
> open from from 12.00-19.15; closed 30 Oct-1 May, also Mon outside high season €€-€€€
>
> **traditional food, wood fire cooked, or snacks by the pool**
>
> **chef's suggestions every evening and Sunday lunch**
>
> **entrées:** regional charcuterie (photo page 8); 'the Restonica salad' (green salad, *panzetta* and *figatellu*, tomatos, nuts, *fromage frais*); Corsican soup (see page 102); *brocciu* and mint omelette
>
> **fish:** small trout filets — plain, with Corsican herbs, or with garlic; scallops wrapped in pancetta *en brochette* with a leek and cream sauce; 'sea trio' of scallops, squid and prawns in a cream sauce with pasta
>
> **meat:** milk-fed lamb; fillets and faux-fillets with roquefort or pepper sauce or flambéed in *eau de vie*; wild boar stew with fresh pasta; Corsican veal
>
> **desserts:** hot apple pie with ice cream (to order at start of meal); parfait with *brocciu*, chestnut and vanilla ice cream, chestnut sauce and whipped cream; Corsican cheese with fig chutney (see page 32)
>
> the excellent **wine** list offers choices of all Corsican wines listed by region

If you don't like garlic, give this dish a miss. But remember that roasted garlic has a mild, almost sweet taste.

Roast leg of lamb with garlic *(gigot d'agneau roti)*

Preheat the oven to 190°C/375°F/gas mark 5. Blanche the garlic and onion for a minute in boiling water (and parboil any another other vegetables you may like to *roast* with the meat), then pan dry and brush lightly with olive oil. Rub the lamb all over with olive oil (again, use a light touch!). Make small incisions in the meat and insert a few slivers of garlic, distributing them evenly.

Place the onion and garlic in the bottom of a roasting pan, then put in a rack and place the meat on top. Roast for 20-25min, or until the meat starts to brown. Now pour over the wine, and continue roasting, basting once or twice, until the meat thermometer registers 140° for medium-rare. Total cooking time should be 2-1/2h but, if you prefer your lamb pink, it should be done in 2h.

Ingredients (for 4 people)
- 1.5 kg leg of lamb
- 40 (yes 40!) whole garlic cloves (about 8 full heads)
- 2 red onions, quartered
- 1 tsp Corsican herbs
- 150 ml red wine
- salt, freshly ground black pepper
- 2 tbsp olive oil

Let the meat sit for 10min before carving and add the meat juices to the pan — you may want to boil them up for a few minutes to scrape up all the crunchy bits and reduce. Add more wine if you don't have enough liquid, and reduce again.

recipes

eat

Grilled sea bass with fennel (loup de mer grillé au fenouil)

The *auberge* serves their grilled bass covered with poached fennel, but with a sort of hot vegetable 'relish' on the side (see photograph). To make life easier, we've incorporated all the fennel into the relish; serve it atop or beside the fish.

Wash the vegetables. Cut the fennel, leeks and onions into disks 1 cm thick. Pop the leeks, onions, tomatoes and peppers into boiling salted water for a minute or two, then drain and dry.

Quickly fry all the vegetables in a little oil until they just begin to colour. Add the fennel seeds and the chopped herbs and seasoning. Mix well and let this simmer for about 10min. If it begins to dry out, add a little white wine.

While the vegetables are simmering, grill the fish, whole, for about 5min on each side. Carefully transfer the fish to warm plates and serve with the vegetable relish and rice.

Ingredients (for 4 people)
4 small sea bass (about 300 g each) — either packaged or gutted by your fishmonger
4 fennel bulbs
1 leek
12 cherry tomatoes, whole
1/4 each yellow, red and green peppers, finely diced
12 spring onions
8 cloves of garlic
40 ml olive oil
30 ml or so of white wine
1 tsp fennel seeds
2 tbsp each chopped chervil, dill, flat parsley
salt, freshly-ground black pepper

Long a favourite spot for trout fishermen and swimmers, up until 1905 the Cascades d'Aitone also powered three mills for grinding chestnut flour — once a staple of the local diet, and still used today in the better restaurants. This short walk is a delight of waterfalls glistening through a mixed wood of pine, fir, yew and beech.

cascades d'aitone
WALK 8

cascades d'aitone **walk 8**

view southwest over Evisa

The walk from Evisa descends into the Spelunca Gorge from the southern edge of the village, then climbs to Ota, but transport is a major problem. Instead we have chosen this easy route, readily accessible by car. If you're full of energy, there are *three* routes to tackle, in close proximity, before you make your way to Evisa for a meal.

Start out at the **'EVI 05' signpost** (❶), where the Mare à Mare Nord briefly joins the D84. Opposite, at the left of a copper-coloured 'Evisa' sculpture, follow the track behind the barrier (orange waymarks) to a picnic area with tables. Now steps take you down to the **Piscine d'Aitone** (**15min**), a good picnicking and swimming spot.

Keeping to the left (south) side of the **Ruisseau d'Aitone**, now follow the rough path (agility required) beside the

Distance: 2.3km/1.4mi; 1h

Grade: easy, but you must be agile. Descent/ascent of 90m/300ft. *IGN map 4150 OT*

Equipment: as page 12; strong shoes, bathing things

Transport: 🚗 to/from roadside parking by fire-point sign 'EVI 05' on the side of the D84 north of Evisa (42° 15.792'N, 8° 49.473'E)

Extension: Chemin des Châtaigniers (6km/3.7mi; 2h15min). Our *very* short walk is just part of a longer version that starts in Evisa (❸) at 42° 15.252'N, 8° 48.234'E, with information panels.

Alternative walk: Sentier de la Sittelle (3.2km/2mi; 1h10min; easy, very little ascent). This nature trail is 3.5km north of the Cascades trail, at a yellow fire-point sign, 'P79' (parking at 42° 16.316'N, 8° 50.719'E). Waymarked with yellow flashes and wooden posts bearing a *sittelle* motif (*Sitta Whiteheadi*, the Corsican nuthatch). Beautiful walk through firs and Corsican pines; picnic tables. See map.

Refreshments:
hotel-restaurant in Evisa (see recommendation on page 80); *none en route*

Points of interest:
waterfalls, rock pools, Aitone River
old mills

77

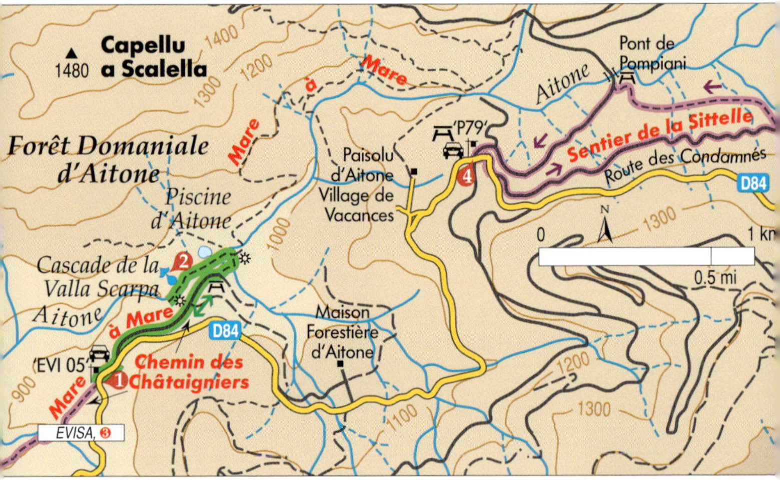

cascading river as far as the signpost '**fin de sentiero balisée**'. From here you have a fine view of the largest waterfall, the **Cascade de la Valla Scarpa** (❷; **30min**). One of the mills stood here; now there are only some walls and two millstones.

Return the same way, passing two more **ruined mills**, to the **'EVI 05' sign** on the D84 (❶; **1h**). From here the 'Chestnut Trail' continues southwest to Evisa (❸): you could follow it into the village for lunch, then return to your car. Or you could first drive north to the Sentier de la Sittelle (❹) …

The *sittelle* waymarking posts

cascades d'aitone **walk 8**

Cascades d'Aitone

L'Aitone

On our first visit to L'Aitone, we spent a few nights — in mid-November. Dinner was served in the 'snug' with fireplace — so cosy! It was our first experience of wild boar stew, and it has never tasted better... Our next visit was on a rainy October day, just for lunch: the friendly restaurant was very warm and welcoming, brightened by rose-coloured place mats and 'Provençal'-style tablecloths. Eventually we managed to visit on a day when the weather was fine and we could take in the fantastic views on offer from the panoramic dining room and the terrace.

Menus vary with the season; rabbit happened to be on the menu for our October visit, and it was a superb warmer. They had beautiful roast potatoes, but we choose the polenta, which was served in the same wine sauce as the rabbit.

> **L'AITONE**
> D 84, Evisa (04 95 26 20 04
> www.hotel-aitone.com
> closed Dec-Feb and Mon lunch €–€€
>
> the **menu touristique** at 23 € is limited: a vegetable entrée, Aitone trout or Corsican omelette (with *brocciu*), vegetables, dessert
>
> the **menu terroir** at 28 € offers a choice of three entrées, two mains and dessert
>
> the **menu mer** at 32 € features salmon carpaccio, fillet of bream with fennel, dessert
>
> there are **chef's suggestions** (à la carte) — perhaps John Dory with aïoli and vegetables, wild boar and polenta, veal sauté with ceps, filet of pork in curry sauce with minced ginger and rice

Fried maize polenta at L'Aitone. Chestnut polenta is also popular on the island, but not usually fried.

Rabbit sautéed with ceps
(lapin sauté aux cèpes)

Preheat the oven to 190°C/375°F/gas mark 5. If you are using dried mushrooms, soak them in warm water for about 30min.

Brown the rabbit pieces in the oil in a heavy casserole, then set aside. Reduce the heat and gently fry the bacon bits, onions and mushrooms until golden. Set aside.

Deglaze the casserole with the wine and stir in the tomato concentrate. Put the meat and mushroom mixture back in, add the thyme, bay, garlic cloves, salt and pepper. Stir to mix. The liquid should just cover the meat (if it does not, add more wine!).

Cover the casserole and cook for 50min-1h, by which time the meat should be falling off the bone. If the sauce is too thin for your taste, strain it into a saucepan and boil rapidly to reduce. Pour over the meat and sprinkle with parsley. Serve with fried polenta (as shown opposite).

Ingredients (for 4 people)

- 1.5 kg rabbit, jointed
- 500 g fresh ceps (porcini mushrooms), or 150 g dry, roughly sliced
- 2 onions, diced
- 100 g diced streaky bacon, unsmoked
- 1 bay leaf
- 2 springs fresh thyme
- 4 garlic cloves, unpeeled
- 1 tbsp tomato concentrate
- 300 ml red wine (or use half chicken stock)
- 2-3 tbsp olive oil
- 2 tbsp chopped flat parsley
- salt and pepper

recipes

The 'Sentier du Littoral des Agriates' is a 40km-long coastal path stretching from St-Florent to Ostriconi Beach. The land was bought in the 1990s — after fierce opposition and many judicial reviews — by the Conservatoire du Littoral and has been developed and managed for the enjoyment of walkers and others.

sentier du littoral
WALK

Ruined Genoese tower at Punta Mortella

Whether you follow the whole route suggested here, or only stroll for an hour or so, then stop and swim, this is a lovely walk. Consider driving to the Anse de Fornali to begin: despite all the negotiations and judicial reviews, the wealthy landowners between St-Florent and this cove have managed to bar walkers from their properties which stretch right down to the shore — with jetties, boathouses, and the like. So for the first hour or so, we have to follow a dusty track *behind* their land.

Our walk starts in the centre of **St-Florent** (**❶**): follow the main **D81 towards l'Ile-Rousse**. At the port, take the **footbridge** (**❷**) to the far side of the **Aliso River** and walk across the sandy **Plage de la Roya** to the end. From the end of the beach head inland; then, almost immediately, turn right up a narrow lane, onto a dirt road (**❸**; **25min**). After a dusty, boring 35 minutes,

Distance: up to 20km/12.4mi; 6h20min *from St-Florent*; 13km/8mi; 4h20min *from the Anse de Fornali*. *Allow plenty of extra time – up to 9h!*

Grade: easy ups and downs on a good coastal path (about 300m/1000ft over the entire 20km), but virtually *no shade. IGN map 4348 OT*

Equipment: as page 12; stout shoes, *adequate sun protection is essential,* bathing things and *plenty of water* recommended

Transport: 🚗 to/from St-Florent or the Anse de Fornali (42° 41.288'N, 9° 16.371'E). By car you can drive along the walking route as far as the 1h-point, saving 2h out-and-back. The tracks are bumpy, so check your insurance for tyre damage liability, unless you're in a 4WD vehicle. 🚐 There are buses from Bastia and l'Ile-Rousse, but times are inconvenient at present. See page 133.

Refreshments:
bars, cafés, restaurants at St-Florent (see page 87); *none en route*

Points of interest:
coastal flora and fauna
creeks and sandy beaches

walk & eat CORSICA

you'll arrive above the **Anse de Fornali** (❹; **1h**), where the walk proper begins. Here you'll find a signpost for the **Sentier du Littoral**. From the parking area head down to the coastal path.

Heading west, you pass below some exquisite properties (some of Europe's wealthiest families have properties here). But

sentier du littoral **walk 9**

Anse de Fornali, with clouds above Cap Corse

your attention will be no doubt be drawn to the wild flowers, the cloud patterns over Cap Corse, and the endless expanse of crystal-clear aquamarine sea. Just walk as far as you like; stop to botanise or swim — preferably in a little inlet all your own.

Landmarks are the sandy beach at the mouth of the **Fiume Bughiu** (**5**; **2h**) and the fjord-like inlet at the **Fiume Santu** (**6**; **2h20min**), where you'll probably have to wade in waist-high water! From here it's another 50 minutes to the **Punta Mortella**, with its old **Genoese watchtower** (**7**; **3h10min**). (Nelson was so impressed when his fleet attacked this very tower in 1794 that the so-called Martello towers in Kent and Sussex were built and

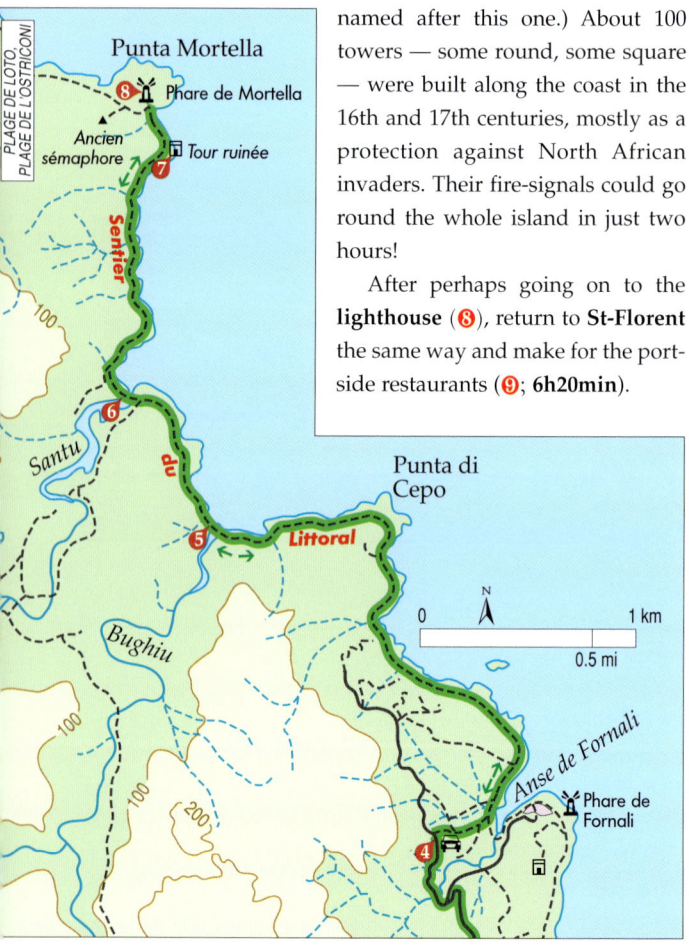

named after this one.) About 100 towers — some round, some square — were built along the coast in the 16th and 17th centuries, mostly as a protection against North African invaders. Their fire-signals could go round the whole island in just two hours!

After perhaps going on to the **lighthouse** (**8**), return to **St-Florent** the same way and make for the portside restaurants (**9**; **6h20min**).

restaurant • **u furnellu**

L'Olivier

Our favourite restaurant in St-Florent — indeed, one of our all-time favourites on the island — closed several years ago, and its successor wasn't really up to scratch. Now a totally new place has opened at the same address, and we must confess: we've not been there — it opened after our last trip to St-Florent.

We read that the restaurant is No 2 of 45 on Trip Advisor(!) and can't wait to visit when next checking walks around St-Florent. Everything at l'Olivier is beautifully presented, and you have a wonderful view of the port and mountains. (Of course, you could say that about *any* of the quayside restaurants, but we still think it is in *the* best location.)

For now, however, we still offer recipes from our original 'find' on the pages overleaf.

L'OLIVIER
Port de Plaisance, Saint-Florent
restaurant-lolivier.fr
Apr-Nov, daily, from 12.00-14.00 and 19.00-22.00 €€-€€€
(04 95 37 08 46

menu or menu corse at 26€ for 3 couses

the **speciality** is crêpes — from a 3-cheese crêpe with Roquefort to a sweet one filled with Corsican clementine jam and whipped cream

entrées include carpaccio of swordfish, Corsican charcuterie

salads like buratta with multi-coloured mini tomatoes; *salade de copines* (chicken, avocado, boiled egg, greens, radishes, tomatoes)

various types of **pasta**, with perhaps prawns or carbonara

for **fish** there is filet of John Dory served with a separate sauce in a little saucepan or *fritto misto* (deep-fried prawns, fish, squid, clams) with chips and 2 different sauces

meats include *wok de poulet aux légumes* — chicken and diced vegetables prettily served in a tiny wok; filet steak with sauce of choice, filet of veal in mushroom sauce

desserts include chestnut-based sweets with sauce or whipped cream — a reminder of the 'Le Petit Napoléon' on page 89

restaurants

eat

TWO WAYS WITH MUSSELS

Provençal-style *(moules à la provençale)*, pictured

Simplicity itself — especially if you have a serving dish as shown here. Allow 12 small mussels per person. Open them, clean them, and keep the largest shells. Place the shells in the heatproof serving dish, a mussel in each shell. Mince a bunch of parsely and 4 garlic cloves; mix well and sprinkle over the mussels. (Some recipes call for 1 tbsp breadcrumbs to be added to the parsley mix.) Then pour over olive oil or melted butter and grill for about 5-6min. Serve with lemon wedges — and perhaps pieces of tomato for colour.

<u>Corsican-style: ingredients (for 4 people)</u>

- 1 kg mussels
- 2 tomatoes, skinned, de-seeded and cubed
- 1 onion, finely sliced
- 3 garlic cloves
- 1 bunch parsley, chopped
- 1 bay leaf
- 1 sprig of thyme
- olive oil
- salt and pepper
- 1 tbsp bread crumbs

Corsican-style *(moules à la mode corse)*, not pictured

Clean the mussels and place them in a heavy casserole with very little water. Heat over a high flame just until they open, then remove and drain. Strain the juice and set aside.

Gently fry the onions, garlic and parsley for 5min. Then add the tomatoes, thyme and bay. Simmer for about 20min. Pour in the reserved liquid; add the mussels and season.

The sauce should be fairly thick; if it is not, add the level tbsp of breadcrumbs. Simmer for another 5min before serving.

'Petit Napoléon'

This recipe made a knock-out dessert at our favourite place, and it's gluten-free. On the Olivier website there is a photo of something very similar, but it is not identified. Let's hope!

If you are using dried chestnuts, soak them overnight and cook until tender (about an hour). If using fresh, boil them for a few minutes, skin them, then boil for about another 20 minutes.

Preheat the oven to 160°C/325°F/gas mark 3. Prepare a loose-bottomed 20 cm/8 in circular cake tin by greasing thoroughly. (If you use a bread tin, as shown here, getting it out may pose a problem!)

Cream the chestnuts in a blender (if you don't have one, mash them *very* finely with whatever is to hand…) Stir in the apples and walnuts. In a separate container, beat the egg yolks and sugar; add the baking powder and vanilla. Add this mixture to the chestnut purée.

Beat the egg whites until they form soft peaks, then gently fold into the cake mixture.

Cook the cake in the preheated oven for 35min, or until a skewer inserted into the middle comes out clean.

Ingredients (for 10 servings)

200 g fresh or prepared chestnuts
50 g chopped walnuts
50 g apples, finely chopped
125 g granulated sugar
4 eggs, separated
1 tsp baking powder
1 tsp vanilla

To serve (optional)
melted dark chocolate
whipped cream

The Plage de l'Ostriconi lies at the western end of the Sentier du Littoral des Agriates (Walk 9). It's one of the few areas of dunes in Corsica and a textbook habitat for plants and birds. The setting is magnificent: the river meanders through rich farmlands and trees to its mouth at the vivid turquoise sea, collared by white sand dunes.

ostriconi
WALK 10

osticoni walk 10

Ostriconi Beach and the Désert des Agriates

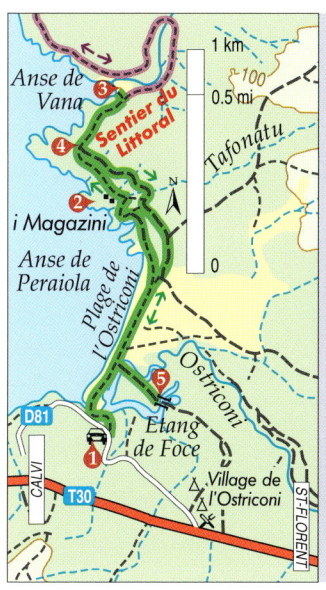

Distance: 4.8km/3mi; 1h45min

Grade: easy after a *very steep, rough descent (ladder!)*; be prepared to wade; *no shade*. IGN map 4249 OT

Equipment: as page 12; sun protection, bathing things, *drinks aplenty*

Transport: 🚗 to/from the Village de l'Ostriconi, a campsite on the old (disused) D81, 2.5km west of the Ile-Rousse/St-Florent junction; park near the path down to the beach (42° 39.492'N, 9° 3.555'E). Or park at the campsite's restaurant and walk from there. 🚌: from l'Ile-Rousse; as Walk 9, page 83.

Refreshments: restaurant at the Village de l'Ostriconi (see page 93); *none en route*

Points of interest: dune habitat and the beach

The walk begins at the **parking bays** (❶) above the beach. Scramble down one of the steep paths, then (outside summer) wade across the mouth of the **Ostriconi River**. Cross the **Plage de l'Ostriconi** and, on the far side, rise up on a track; then fork left on the coastal path. After crossing a streambed, the path runs above two small **ruins** (❷; **i Magazini**) and then between two old stone pillars (navigational aids). You can end the outgoing walk at the **Anse de Vana** (❸; **45min**) with a swim, or follow the continuing path as far as you like.

walk & eat CORSICA

On your return take the **sandy inland track** (❹; waymarked with an arrow carved in stone). Pass a signboard for the **Sentier du Littoral** (**1h10min**). A few minutes later, at a Y-fork, turn down right to the beach. Walk along the back of the beach until you come to a juniper- and reed-edged creek. Follow the cart track beside it (be prepared to wade) to a little **footbridge** (❺) over the **Etang de Foce**. This is an idyllic spot, with eucalyptus and farmland on the far side — and the Village de l'Ostriconi, a lovely place to spend a holiday in the wooden bungalows or campsite. Then return across the beach and climb up to the **parking bays** (❶; **1h 45min**).

Have a meal at the restaurant at the Village de l'Ostriconi, or, if it's out of season, drive on to l'Ile-Rousse or St-Florent.

ostriconi **walk 10**

VILLAGE DE L'OSTRICONI
2.5km west of the Ile-Rousse/St-Florent junction on the T30
(04 95 60 10 05
www.village-ostriconi.com
closed from 10/10 till 1/05, otherwise open all day €€

full **breakfasts**

large choice of **entrées**, **salads**, **pastas**, **omelettes**, **pizzas** for a light meal.

fish and **seafood**, **steaks**, **veal**, **chicken**

small wine list

Ostriconi

This very attractive restaurant is just as up-market as the 3-star holiday village/campsite: one of the sweets was 'chocolate soup with a cinnamon infusion, vanilla-roasted apple slices, and croutons of carmelised spiced bread'! In summer, bar and barbecues on the terrace by the pool.

restaurants
eat

One of the best times to take this delightful ramble is late in the day, when you can sit by the chapel watching the fishing boats, yachts and high-speed ferries making for the port below Calvi's citadel under the setting sun. On the other hand, early mornings are cool (for the climb) and you'll have plenty of time for a swim.

notre-dame de la serra
WALK

notre-dame de la serra **walk 11**

The walk starts at the **railway station** in **Calvi** (**1**): walk up steps to the main street (Avenue de la République), cross it, and turn left. Now take the first turn to the right (a wide trunk road, in front of the pharmacy). Then take the first left (signpost '**stade**'). Turn right in front of the **stadium** (**2**), then go left beside it (sign: '**EDF**'). Follow this road to the EDF building on the right and, 100m further on watch for a small sign '**Notre-Dame de la Serra**' at the right of the entrance to **Villa de Iris** on your left (**3**; **15min**).

This sign directs you along a short passage leading to a climb over smooth rock with some steps. You rise to a field, where you can see the chapel, Notre-Dame de la Serra, ahead. Take the clear, *maquis*-lined footpath just to the left of the field. Sporadic orange and red waymarks take you

---

Distance: 8.5km/5.3mi; 2h10min

Grade: fairly easy ascent/descent of 200m/650ft on good tracks and paths. *IGN map 4149 OT*

Equipment: as page 12; stout shoes, sun protection, bathing things

Transport: 🚂, 🚌 or 🚗 to/from Calvi's railway station

Longer walk: la Revellata (16km/10mi; 4h10min; grade as main walk, but quite long). Follow the main walk to the Plage de l'Alga (**5**; 1h30min), then go *left* on the coastal path. Beyond the largest cove (Anse de l'Oscelluccia), the path rises and eventually climbs to the road to the old lighthouse (**8**). Turn right to the lighthouse at the end of the point. You could continue 0.5km to the Marine Biology Research Centre (**9**): it's private property, but access on foot is allowed. If you would like to visit, arrange it in advance (stareso.com/access/php; ✆ 06 86 22 32 61). Return the same way to the Plage d'Alga and pick up the main walk again.

Refreshments:
bars, cafés, restaurants in Calvi
seasonal bar/café at the Plage de l'Alga

Points of interest:
Notre-Dame de la Serra; viewpoint la Revellata seascapes

all the way to the chapel, **Notre-Dame de la Serra** (**4**; **50min**).

Leave the chapel by heading due west — on the access road or the walkers' track to the right; 10 minutes down you pass some fascinating rocks *(tafoni)*. When the road/track forks, keep right and come to the main D81b (**Porto road**; **1h10min**). Turn left here and, almost immediately turn right on the track to the lighthouse on **la Revellata**. Soon you can take any of the paths or tracks down to the little cove below to the right (there are usually signs here, with the word '**bar**' pointing the way). When you arrive at the **Plage de l'Alga** (**5**; **1h30min**), indulge in a swim and some refreshment at the bar (only open in high season).

If you are full of energy (or have a date with the Marine Biology Research Centre), now make for the lighthouse. Otherwise, follow the wide footpath from here along the coast towards Calvi. The path ends at a junction: turn right uphill on a **lane** (**6**). You pass holiday bungalows on the right in about five minutes, then come to the coastal

notre-dame de la serra walk 11

road to Porto (**D81b**; ⑦) by the entrance to Résidence Tramariccia. Turn left on the main road and follow it past U Fanale (see page 99) and the **citadel**, back to the **railway station** in **Calvi** (❶; 2h10min).

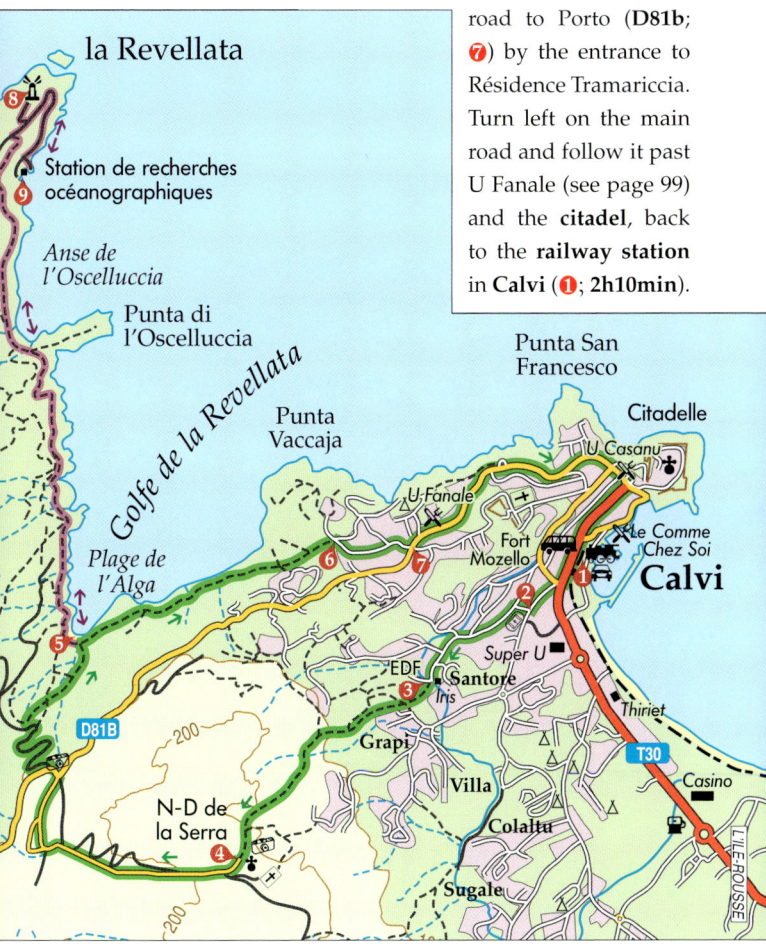

La Revellata: the Marine Biology Research Centre and old lighthouse

U Fanale

This restaurant, just 150m the Calvi side of where the walk comes back to the Porto road after the Résidences Tramariccia, is named for its view to the setting opposite — the Revellata lighthouse *(fanale)*. There is a terrace, too — rather like being in the bow of a ship looking out to sea.

The à la carte dishes are expensive, but there are two economical 3-course *menus* — one at 30 € and a 'Menu Corse' at 36 €. Not all the dishes shown opposite will always be available: our mini-menu is just intended to show the imaginative variety.

The presentation of the food matches the menu: their risotto with crayfish is shown on page 104 — truly a work of art, *and* it was superb. Our only complaint was that, sitting indoors, upstairs, the food was not hot enough … but *no* restaurants on Corsica seem to warm plates …

U FANALE
Route de Porto, Calvi
(04 95 65 18 82
instagram.com/ufanalecalvi/?hl=en-gb (also a page on Facebook)
open from 15 Apr until 14 Oct, daily (ex Tue lunch) in high season, then Thu-Sat evenings, Sun lunch and dinner €€€

entrées like *salade du pêcheur* (giant prawns, crayfish, scallops); terrine of salmon and swordfish; tart of Corsican *coppa* (see page 8); *Corsican* charcuterie; 'melt' of warm goats' cheese *(chevre)*; fish soup; Corsican soup (recipe page 102)

pastas include salmon in tagliatelli or with pan-fried giant prawns

fish: locally-caught swordfish with a little tomato and thyme tart and sweet pepper chutney; daurade in a mille-feuille pastry; risotto with crayfish (recipe page 104)

wide range of **omelettes**

meats: rumpsteak with cognac and mushroom sauce; lamb in a crispy-skin with rosemary-flavoured olives and a sweet garlic cream; duck breast with fritters *(beignets)*, figs and *foie gras*; veal escalope in cream sauce

sweets: fiadone (recipe page 123); fruit with Corsican muscat wine; *mi-cuit au chocolat noir* (individual puddings made with dark chocolate, sugar, eggs, butter and a bit of flour)

restaurants

eat

U Casanu

If you're not 'in the know', and you make straight for the port, you may walk past this *minuscule* restaurant without even seeing it. But once you've eaten there, you'll return again and again,

Octopus on a sizzle platter

until you have worked your way through the menu!

When we first discovered U Casanu the chef was Japanese! But that didn't stop him from serving 100 per cent Corsican dishes, perfectly cooked. The owner finally retired, having run the restaurant for 30 or more years; the new owners have completely redecorated but kept many of the dishes that we so love — and it seems that you do too: the place goes from strength to strength.

> **U CASANU**
> 18 Boulevard Wilson, Calvi
> (04 95 65 00 10; open daily for lunch and dinner; €€-€€€
>
> **specialities** are either octopus (shown here) or lamb, first cooked for 4 hours to perfect tenderness, then served with a 'ratatouille' of roasted vegetables, much as sown here with the octopus
>
> also **authentic Corsican food**: *suppa corse* (recipe overleaf), *figatellu* (pork liver sausage) with eggs, fantastic *al dente* pastas, Corsican charcuterie, *bouillabaisse* with sardines and saffron, local fish and seafood, duck, an unusual cassoulet, *stuffatu* (recipe page 103), *carpaccio* of salmon
>
> Orsini **wines** (the vineyard on the road to Calenzana)

restaurants

eat

Le Comme Chez Soi

We return to this restaurant again and again. Some of the other quayside restaurants (we always want to be where the 'action' is)

> **LE COMME CHEZ SOI**
> Quai Landry ℂ 04 95 33 84 70
> instagram.com/lecommechezsoicalvi
> closed Nov-Apr, otherwise open
> daily for lunch and dinner €€-€€€
>
> **'menu corse'** at only 25.50 € for 3 courses, with a 3-way choice for each (fish, meat, vegetarian)
>
> 13 **entrées**, from the usual plate of Corsican meats or fish soup to parslied frogs legs (seldom seen on Corsican menus) or a 'Buddha salad' with Oriental overtones
>
> 13 **main courses**, including
>
> a **fish** speciality (the daurade shown here); risotto with prawns
>
> large choice of **meats**, from duck leg confit, sweetbreads, shoulder of Corsican lamb, suckling pig, beef, veal; there is even a hamburger of minced Corsical veal
>
> 8 **sweets** to die for — including a very unusual pavlova with apples, strawberries and mascarpone
>
> good selection of Corsican **wines**

Daurade in a herb crust with vegetables in a coriander and soya sauce

have limited or (for us) 'boring' menus, but Le Comme Chez Soi has always catered for a very wide range of tastes. For the last several years it has been under new ownership, with special emphasis on 'bio' and local produce.

We *could* have dined quite inexpensively with the Menu Corse, but we treated ourselves to the courgette fritters and tomato with buffala mozzarella, then went on to the daurade, followed by melon 'soup' and everyone's favourite — the pavlova…

It's lovely being here, part of the lively marina-side atmosphere, from the first apéritif to the post-prandial coffee and brandy!

Traditional Corsican soup *(suppa corsa)*

Soak the beans overnight (or cheat and use tinned!). Cut the cabbage into wedges and the potatoes into large cubes. Slice the carrots thickly and quarter the tomatoes. Mince the chard, onions and garlic.

Ingredients (for 4 people)
- 1 bone of dry Corsican (or similar) ham, with some meat
- 1/2 small cabbage
- 250 g Swiss chard (or pak choi)
- 3 waxy potatoes
- 1 carrot
- 2 onions
- 2 tomatoes
- 200 g dry haricot beans
- 150g macaroni
- 2 garlic cloves, crushed
- 2 tbsp olive oil
- 2 l water
- salt and pepper
- fresh basil and marjoram, minced

Heat the oil in a large, deep heavy-bottomed saucepan and cook the vegetables for about 3min, untill golden. Then pour over the water, add the beans and put in the ham bone. *(If you are using tinned beans, add them just 10min before cooking finishes.)*

Bring to the boil, then turn down and leave it to just lightly bubble for about 2h, skimming when necessary. Season halfway through the cooking, remembering that the ham is already salty!

About 10min before the vegetables are cooked, add the beans if tinned, and macaroni. The latter is optional (some recipes call for stale bread instead), but remember, this is intended to be a *very* thick soup. Stir in the minced herbs at the last minute.

Meat stew with smoked ham (stuffatu)

If you are using dry mushrooms, soak them in some warm water (for about 30min). Cut all the meat into cubes, dice the ham, mince the onions and crush the garlic.

In a heavy-bottomed casserole, fry all the above (except the mushrooms) in olive oil for about 10min, turning to brown all sides. Pour in the wine, and stir in the tomato paste. Add the mushrooms, bouquet garni, and salt and pepper to taste.

Bring everything to the boil, then lower the heat and cook on top of the hob for about 2h30min-3h, until the meat is meltingly tender.

On Corsica, of course this stew is served with pasta (usually tagliatelli), but it is equally good with mashed or boiled potatoes.

> The ubiquitous *salade bergère* (shown below at La Cave, l'Ile-Rousse) pops up on all menus. Easy to make at home, it contains grilled cheese (*brocciu* or *chevre*) on bread, Corsican ham(s), tomatoes, pickles, and other ingredients to taste — perhaps peppers, cucumber, raw mushrooms, raisins, pine nuts, walnuts, black olives, figs or fig chutney. All served on a bed of *very fresh* lettuce, in a vinaigrette sweetened with a delicate Corsican honey rather than sugar.

Ingredients (for 4 people)
- 400 g beef (shoulder)
- 400 g lamb (shoulder)
- 250 g *prizuttu* (prosciutto), sliced fairly thick
- 400 g fresh ceps (porcini mushrooms), or 100 g dry mushrooms
- 2 onions
- 3 cloves of garlic
- 0.5 l red wine
- 1 bouquet garni
- 1 level tbsp tomato paste
- olive oil
- salt and pepper

Ingredients (for 4 people)
- 350 g arborio rice
- 350 g cooked, shelled *langoustines* (Dublin Bay prawns), cut into bite-sized pieces
- 4 whole *langoustines*, unshelled
- 600 ml fish stock
- 150 ml dry white wine
- 4 spring onions, sliced (including the green tops)
- 1/2 green pepper, diced
- 1/2 red pepper, diced
- salad greens, like *mesclun*
- 2 lemons
- 3-4 tbsp olive oil
- salt and pepper
- optional: grapes, flowers and pastry fantasies to decorate!

Langoustine risotto (risotto aux langoustines)

Well, we are not going to show you our version of this dish when we can show you U Fanale's for inspiration! It tasted as good as it looked. If Dublin Bay prawns elude you, use readily-available tiger prawns.

In a medium heavy skillet, gently fry the onions and peppers in some oil for a few minutes, until golden. Pour in the wine and leave to simmer on the lowest heat. Just a few minutes before the rice (see below) has finished cooking, put the prawns, including the four in their shells (used later to decorate), into this wine mixture and heat through.

Meanwhile, warm 2 tbsp of oil in a large heavy-bottomed skillet. Add the rice and stir constantly for a couple of minutes. Then add the stock a little at a time, always stirring, until all the liquid is taken up and the rice is tender and creamy (about 20min).

Gently stir in the prawn and wine mixture and decorate quickly, to serve piping hot!

recipes

eat

Pork and chestnut terrine *(terrine de porc aux châtaignes)*

Put the minced shallot in a dish and just cover with oil; set aside. Take 5 outside cabbage leaves and boil them in salted water for 1min; drain, *dry* and set aside. Finely chop the rest of the cabbage (about 400 g), cook for 10min, then drain, *dry* and set aside.

Fry the pork loins in a little oil just to stiffen and shrink them (or they will shrink too much in the terrine). In a bowl, mix the pork mince, chopped cabbage, shallot, chestnuts, myrtle leaves, cognac, eggs and salt and pepper to taste. *Quickly fry a small ball of this mixture to check the seasoning!*

Preheat the oven to 180°C/350°F/gas mark 4. Line a 2 l earthenware terrine (it must have a lid with a hole) with the bacon strips, then press in a layer of cabbage leaves. Press in half the mixture, *hard* (it will shrink in cooking). Put in a layer of pork loin, trimmed to fit so that it does not overlap. Cover with the rest of the mixture, top with cabbage leaves and bacon strips. Cover.

Put the terrine in a bain-marie or roasting tin with boiling water and cook for about 2h30min-3h, making sure there is always enough *simmering* water. It will be done when a skewer inserted into the centre *for a full half minute* comes out *hot*! Cool at room temperature before serving.

Ingredients (8-16 servings)
- 600 g pork shoulder, roughly minced
- 3 pork loins, deboned, fat trimmed off, pounded to about 1 cm thickness
- 600 g green cabbage
- 300 g prepared chestnuts, whole
- 1 shallot, minced
- 4 medium eggs, beaten
- 10 wild myrtle leaves
- 1 shot glass cognac
- salt and pepper
- a little sunflower oil
- 250 g finely sliced *panzetta* (to line the terrine)

Discover the enchanting villages of the Balagne on foot. This 'starter' walk can be done in either direction (perhaps depending on whether you will have lunch or dinner at one of our restaurants), or as a very short circuit. But by using the notes and maps for Walk 13, you *could* do a 21km-long 'grand tour' — from Lumio to l'Ile-Rousse.

lumio, occi & lavatoggio

WALK 12

Occi: the church has been restored

From Lavatoggio to Lumio: **Start the walk** at the D71 in **Lavatoggio** (❶). Climb the steps just west of the **church** (at the left of a childrens' playground). At the top, turn right on **Allée Roger Dassonville** (area map; weight limit sign). Look behind you, across the valley, to the square church tower at Aregno and to Sant' Antonino straddling a hill. Continue up the concrete lane to a tiny chapel, **San Giovanni di Venti** (❷; **15min**).

Now follow the cart track at the left of the chapel, until you come to another chapel, **Notre-Dame de la Stella** (❸; **45min**). Keep straight ahead on the track past this chapel, too. Then, after 50m/yds, you can either take the cart track uphill to the right or continue for another 120m and take the **path** up to the right (it may be waymarked in yellow or faded orange). (Straight ahead is the

Distance: 7km/4.3mi; 2h-2h20min one way

Grade: quite easy, especially from Lavatoggio to Lumio (overall ascent 150m/490ft); from Lumio to Lavatoggio ascent of 255m/835ft. Good tracks and paths throughout, but *no shade*. IGN maps 4149 OT, 4249 OT

Equipment: as page 12; take a sunhat and plenty of water

Transport: 🚗 car to/from Lavatoggio or Lumio, in which case you will have to *walk both ways*. The easiest alternative is to leave your car at Lumio (42° 34.676'N, 8° 50.080'E), take a taxi to Lavatoggio, and walk back to Lumio (easier gradients).

Alternative walk: Occi circuit (5.5km/3.4mi; 2h; moderate ascent/ descent of 255m/835ft). 🚗 to/from the north entrance to Lumio on the T30. Park just inside the road, opposite the hotel A Casa di Mà (42° 34.855'N, 8° 49.944'E). See notes on page 110.

Refreshments:
Just pour M at Lumio *(lunch only!)*, Chez Edgard *(dinner only!)*, unreliable café at Lavatoggio; *none en route*

Points of interest:
ruined village of Occi
views over the coast

walk & eat CORSICA

path to Lumio followed at the end of the Occi circuit (Alternative walk). Ignoring any paths to the right, rise with fine views to Calvi, la Revellata, the Bonifatu mountains, and Capu d'Occi up to the right.

Beyond a pass below Capu d'Occi, the trail descends to the dramatically perched ruins of **Occi** (**4**; **1h20min**). The village — which probably dates from the 15th century or even much earlier — was abandoned in the 19th century, but various donors have supported restoration of the **church**, where services are still held at least once a year. From the church, walk towards a stone wall and then left, ignoring a good path on the right (it goes down to Camping Panoramic on the D71). Round the village to the north, to its **northwest corner** (**5**).

lumio, occi & lavatoggio **walk 12**

Landscape near Notre-Dame de la Stella

Then descend the old stone-laid mule trail (some cairns and waymarks), soon zigzaging down through pink boulders (**6**; the '**Calanche**'). At a fork, take the track to the right. Coming onto a lane, follow it behind the hotel **A Casa di Mà** (**7**; see page 111), then fork left uphill into **Lumio** (**8**; **2h**).

From Lumio to Lavatoggio: **Start out** at **A Casa di Mà** (**7**): take the lane behind the hotel (sign: '**Village d'Occi**'). Yellow (or faded orange) waymarks mark the old mule trail via the rosy boulders of the **Calanche** (**6**) to the abandoned village of **Occi** (**4**; **45min**). From Occi follow the clear cairned and waymarked path ascending southeast — first ignoring a path off left to Capu d'Occi. You rise to a pass below Capu d'Occi, then descend

At the Calanche

across the U-bend of a cart track to a crossing track. Turn left, pass the chapel **Notre-Dame de la Stella** (❸; **1h25min**), then carry on to another, tiny chapel, **San Giovanni di Venti** (❷; **2h05min**). Now keep straight ahead along a concrete lane (**Allée Roger Dassonville**); this takes you down to the **church** at **Lavatoggio** (❶; **2h20min**).

Alternative walk: Occi circuit: **Start** at **A Casa di Mà** (❼): follow the notes for the Lumio to Lavatoggio route to the chapel of **Notre-Dame de la Stella** (❸; **1h 25min**). Turn right here and just keep straight on (due west), to descend quite steeply back to **Lumio** (❽; **2h**).

Just pour M and Chez Edgard

There are restaurants at both ends of this walk, and they are very different. **Just pour M** is the bistro of the hotel A Casa di Mà with a gorgeous terrace and wonderful views. The hotel has another restaurant, Michelin-starred and *very* expensive, but the bistro — only open for breakfast and lunch — welcomes outside guests and one would not feel out of place in walking gear.

> **JUST POUR M**
> T30, Lumio ✆ 04 95 60 61 71
> acasadima.com/en/corsica-restaurant/juste-pour-m
> closed Sun and Nov-Mar €€-€€€
>
> **for example:** cold meats to share 20€; tuna carpaccio 22€; risotto with summer vegetables 22€

> **CHEZ EDGARD**
> D71, Lavatoggio ✆ 04 95 61 70 75
> chez-edgard.fr
> dinner, and only by ✆ reservation, Easter to Oct €€; no bank cards
>
> **specialities:** skewered meat cooked on an open fire – sometimes duck, sometimes lamb, suckling pig (if ordered in advance), veal sautéed with figs and prunes, wild boar (in the hunting season), Corsican soup, *brocciu* fritters, tart with Corsican herbs, chestnut cake
>
> **single menu 45 €**

On the other hand, be prepared to take a hearty appetite to **Chez Edgard** in Lavatoggio. This is an informal *ferme-auberge*, a working farm serving meals of traditional regional dishes. So the menu is limited and meat-based, but you will enjoy some of the best cooking on Corsica: all the food has been raised or cultivated by the family, members of a proud local farming tradition.

The hotel which preceded A Casa di Mà used to show recipes on their website. There was one for a lobster appetizer with citrus dressing. We've adapted it to make a refreshing luncheon salad.

Seafood salad with a citrus vinaigrette
(salade de fruits de mer en vinaigrette d'agrumes)

First make the vinaigrette by mixing all the ingredients except the garlic and onions in a jar with a lid; shake well to mix, and set aside. *Just before serving*, add the garlic and onions and shake again to mix; pour into a serving dish.

At Chez Charles (the hotel that preceded A Casa di Mà) the presentation was spartan and artistic; the only greenery being a few sprigs of rocket. But for a heartier lunch, we opt for the very freshest butterhead lettuce and chicory as a base.

As for the seafood, we like about 500 g of tiger prawns, 250 g fresh crab meat and 250 g lobster. Cold scallops are equally delicious.

A dry white or rosé wine and some crusty bread makes a feast of this meal.

Ingredients (for 4 people)
1 kg mixed cooked seafood
200 g cherry tomatoes
2 basil leaves, torn up
salad greens to taste
for the vinaigrette:
1 tbsp lemon juice
1 tbsp grapefruit juice
2 tbsp orange juice
100 g purée of ripe mangoes
4 tbsp olive oil
salt and pepper
5 g chopped peeled garlic
15 g finely sliced spring onions

Veal sauté with prunes and figs (sauté de veau aux pruneaux et figues)

Our version of this Chez Edgard dish is easily cooked on the hob.

In a heavy-bottomed skillet *(for which you have a lid)*, fry the bacon bits, onions and garlic in oil until golden and set aside. Then brown the veal in hot oil on all sides and set aside.

Mix 1 tbsp oil and 1 tbsp flour to a paste. Pour some stock into the skillet and heat gently, scraping up any flavourful bits. Add the oil/flour paste, stirring all the time, so that it doesn't form lumps. Add the rest of the stock, the wine, and the tomato paste, still stirring. Bring to the boil and add the herbs and spices, dried figs and prunes. Season.

Return the reserved ingredients to the skillet, cover and cook slowly for 1 hour or so, until the meat is tender and the sauce has reduced. Just before serving, you may wish to stir in a shot glass of cognac and flame it.

Ingredients (for 4 people)

- 800 g veal shoulder, rib or tenderloin, cut into large cubes
- 50 g unsmoked bacon bits
- 1 large onion, chopped
- 2 cloves garlic, crushed
- 200 ml veal (or chicken) stock
- 200 ml dry white wine
- 50-100 g each dried figs and prunes, quartered (to taste)
- 1 tbsp tomato paste
- sprig of thyme; 1 bay leaf
- 2 sprigs of flat parsley
- 1 level tbsp Corsican herbs
- 5 juniper berries, crushed
- olive oil for frying
- 1 tbsp flour
- salt and pepper

Together with Walk 12, this short downhill ramble from Sant' Antonino — the most beautiful village in the Balagne — to bustling l'Ile-Rousse, gives you a good overview of the area. But if the weather is cool and breezy, then we heartily recommend the Alternative walk — it's a 'grand tour' in every sense, a really magnificent hike!

sant' antonino & l'île-rousse

WALK

sant' antonino & l'île-rousse **walk 13**

Sant' Antonino — masterpiece of the Balagne

Start out in **Sant' Antonino**, at the village **car park** (❶). But before setting out, be sure to explore the beautiful village and fortify yourself with some lip-puckering fresh-squeezed *lemon* juice at the Cave Antonini (see page 121)!

Then take the dirt track 100m to the left of the **church** (walkers' signposts), heading for a **cemetery** on a rise. At a fork about 200m/yds along, go *right* (the fork to the left *may* be signposted to the Couvent de Corbara). This sandy track is *not* signposted, but it affords better views and avoids an unnecessary climb in full sun from Corbara. You rise over a **pass** and pass a track up to the relay station on **Capu Corbinu** (❷; **15min**). This is a brilliant viewpoint down over Pigna and Corbara, with the Couvent de Corbara in the foreground, backed by the Cima Sant' Angelo.

Distance: 8km/5mi; 2h10min

Grade: easy descent of 450m/1475ft on good tracks and paths. The waymarks are infrequent, but the route is signposted and straightforward. *IGN maps 4149 OT, 4249 OT*

Equipment: as page 12; *sunhat!*

Transport: 🚖 taxi or with friends to Sant' Antonino; return by 🚌 from l'Ile-Rousse (see page 133)

Alternative walk: la Balagne (21km/13mi; 6h; moderate, but long. *Almost no shade*. Overall ascent: 550m/1800ft; descent 650m/2130ft). Follow Walk 12 *from Lumio to Lavatoggio* (page 109). Then use the map or our GPS files; the route is signposted (do not rely on waymarking). Remember that you will always be on a lane or *good* path (old mule trail). Leaving Lavatoggio, follow the road opposite the church down into Croce, then take the first right (a stone-laid alley). Turn left at the chapel just before Cateri: the trail continues from below Chez Léon. Go through Aregno to the Pisan Romanesque Eglise de la Trinité (12C), then climb to Sant' Antonino. Now pick up Walk 13.

Refreshments: plenty in Sant' Antonino and l'Ile-Rousse; *none en route*

Points of interest: Sant' Antonino and l'Ile-Rousse — and the views!

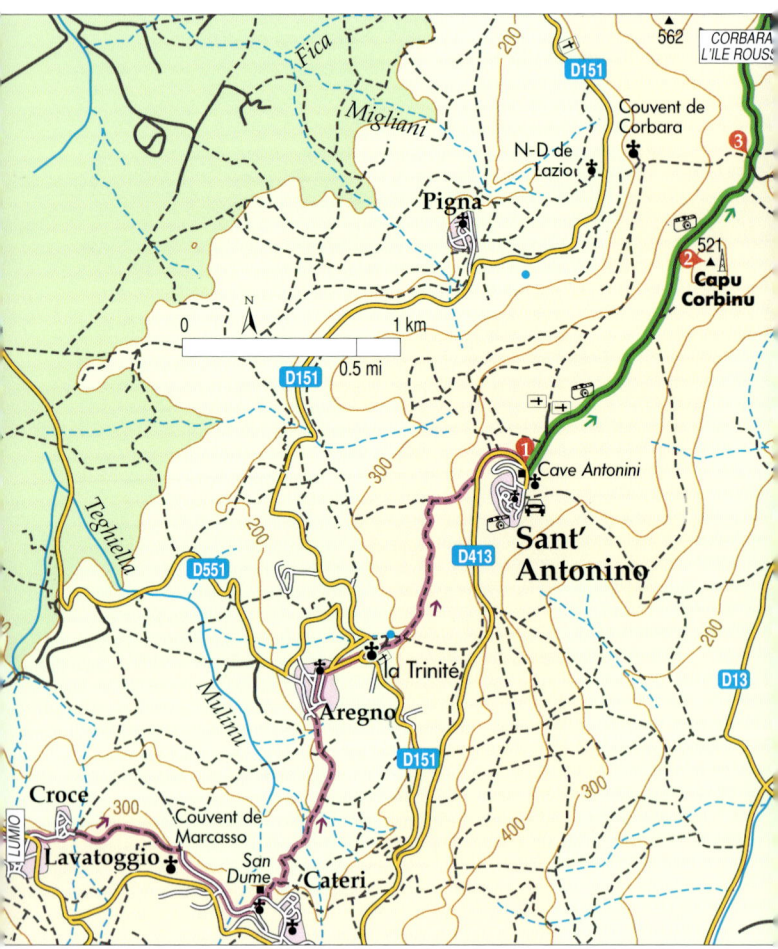

sant' antonino & l'île-rousse **walk 13**

At a T-junction, keep left downhill (**25min**). Two minutes later the **path from the Couvent de Corbara** comes in from the left (❸; there is usually a barrage of signposts at this point, but they are often broken). Keep *right* on the track (you may spot the occasional waymark). As you pass below the **Cima Sant' Angelo** (see map overleaf) you have a good view down to l'Ile-Rousse and its lighthouse; in the middle distance, cypresses and a slender church tower

Approaching Occiglione

announce Occiglioni, the next village en route.

You soon pass a beautiful old **ruined convent** on the right (❹; **40min**). Palmento is the village just below to the east. Be sure to take a break under the venerable oak here — the only shade for miles around! Then follow the track into an S-bend. You'll be surprised when you see that you have *passed* Occiglioni's church! Don't worry, your turn-off back

117

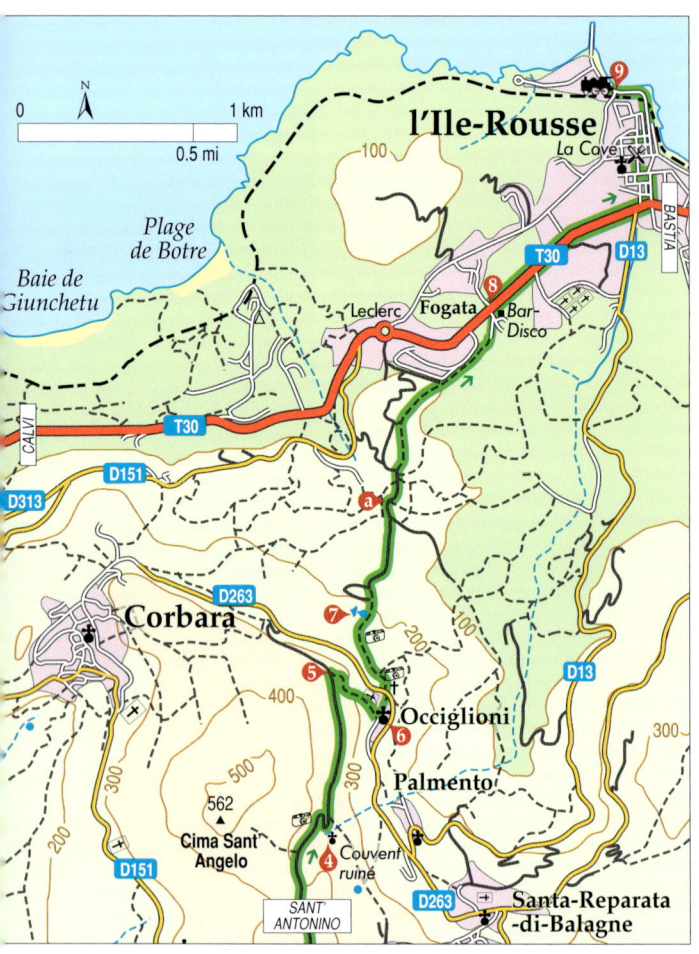

sant' antonino & l'île-rousse **walk 13**

Descending to l'Île-Rousse

to the village comes up 700m/yds past the ruin: take the old mule trail down to the right (**5**; **50min**). Yellow flashes guide you down past the village **cemetery** and **washhouse** (both on the left), and into into **Occiglioni** (**6**; **55min**). Walk to the left of the **church** on a beautifully cobbled path and then follow the cobbles downhill under an arch. Go straight ahead between the houses and in two minutes you come to the D263, by a **viewpoint with an iron cross**.

Go down the concrete steps just to the left of the viewpoint (walkers' signs). Keep left at two Y-forks. From up here you

The plane-shaded square in l'Ile-Rousse is the perfect spot for a break — or have a meal at La Cave, next to the church.

enjoy good views of your final destination. You pass a lovely (but dry!) **fountain** on the left (**7**; **1h 10min**). A few cobbles underfoot remind you that this was once a beautiful old mule trail. But no more: just 20m/yds below the fountain an unpleasant access track has been bulldozed. At least it *was* quite awkward and rutted when last checked, but it was waymarked in yellow almost every metre, so there was no escaping it.

Fifteen minutes down from the fountain you pass a signposted trail off right to 'Ile Rousse' (**a**; just 100m/yds below a track off right signed 'Giro Occiglioni–Palmeto'). We didn't have time to walk this trail (which had been newly cleared), but we think it *might* be a more pleasant route than the 'official' route we take — but it will eventually feed into the D13. Our route rounds a housing development and emerges on the main T30 by **walkers' signposts** (**8**; **1h45min**). Turn right to l'Ile-Rousse; after enjoying some refreshments in the plane-shaded square or a meal, walk on to the **railway station** by the port (**9**; **2h10min**).

juice bar/winery and restaurant • **cave à citron and la cave**

Cave Antonini and La Cave

You're spoilt for choice: there are at least five or six restaurants in Sant' Antonino (but most are closed between October and Easter). We usually start the day by visiting the **Cave Antonini** (open from Easter to 30 Oct) — the large yellow building opposite the car park. This very popular establishment, a village landmark, not only sells lemon juice (you add your own sugar to taste), but almonds (a tonne each year), honey, jams, olive oil and muscat wines (from the Antonini family's neighbouring vineyards). The spotless winery is in a nearby garage.

The Antonini winery and entrées at La Cave

Then we'll walk down to l'Ile-Rousse and have lunch at **La Cave**, a delightful restaurant next to the church, with a pretty outdoor terrace and more tables under the trees. As with most of our chosen restaurants, this place has been family-run for years — but for the last year or two it has been run by a new family…

And, rather like Chez Edgard at Lavatoggio, all their own produce is served. Also like Chez Edgard, there is *no fish* on offer. In fact the menu is quite limited (see overleaf). In its new incarnation, La Cave is run by a brother and sister: she raises livestock and makes cheeses, which he then sells in the restaurant he runs. So they know the provenance of all their dishes.

restaurants

eat

La Cave's tree-shaded seating area across the road from the restaurant (which also has a small terrace at the front). On Google, the restaurant is No 1 of 112 in l'Ile-Rousse.

LA CAVE
Place Paoli (next to the church), l'Ile-Rousse (04 95 58 27 26
lacavebaraviandes.com
open Apr-Nov €€-€€€

as the name implies, a restaurant for meat-eaters; *there is no fish.* Meats from all over the world — like Argentine and American beef … with wines to match.

pizzas and **omelettes** for a lighter meal — or just have an entrée like the Corsican meats platter

entrées include a 'tart of the day', a shepherd's salad like the one shown on page 103, charcuterie and courgette fritters (both shown on page 121)

entrées — veal, lamb and beef, all of which have been raised by the family, but a vegetarian option of cannelloni with *brocciu*

desserts, including chestnut flan and fiadone, as well as cheeses (sheep, cow) from their own dairy

Our photo shows the chestnut cake (left) at the previous incarnation of La Cave and their *fiadone*. We've only given the recipe for the *fiadone* but, if you want to make a truly delicious, pure chestnut cake, then use the recipe on page 89, but *instead of the apples and walnuts,* use 300 g of prepared chestnuts. Preparation method is the same; cooking time will be about 35min.

Fiadone (pictured right)

Preheat the oven to 180°C/350°F/gas mark 4. Beat the eggs and sugar together until fluffy. Crush the *brocciu* with a fork into very fine bits and beat into the egg/sugar mixture with the lemon zest.

Pour into a lined and well-greased, fairly deep 25 cm/9 in pie tin with a removable bottom and bake for 45min, or until a knife inserted into middle comes out clean. As you can see, this is 'cake' does not rise much — it will only be about 2.5 cm high. Let the cake cool in the oven, to avoid the top cracking or caving in.

Tip: To make a lighter *fiadone,* separate the eggs and beat the whites before mixing with the yolks and sugar.

Ingredients (12-16 servings)
500 g *brocciu frais* (or ricotta)
300 g caster sugar
6 eggs
grated rind of one lemon

A train journey into Corsica's interior is a must. Our suggestions — travelling north or travelling south — do not cover the whole route. Instead we take in the most spectacular stretch, allowing you to combine the trip with a short walk and an enjoyable lunch.

'u trinichellu'

EXCURSION

*'u trinichellu' **excursion***

Gustve Eiffel's viaduct above the Vecchio River

The Corsicans affectionately use the diminutive 'little train' ('U Trinichellu') when referring to their narrow-gauge railway … although TGV (Train à Grandes *Vibrations*) is now gaining currency! Tiny it may be, with just two cars, but it is famous round the world.

Like all mountain railways, this was a very difficult project, involving 32 tunnels (one of them 4km long) and 76 bridges and viaducts (including the 140m-long viaduct shown opposite, above the Vecchio River). There used to be another, busy line serving Porto-Vecchio, but it was destroyed by bombing during World War II and never rebuilt.

Rather than describe the route in detail, we highlight and comment briefly on the landmarks in both directions. This is a wonderful day out: you will glide past verdant

Our suggestions: travel north from Ajaccio as far as Corte, or south from Ponte Leccia as far as Vizzavona.

Timings and logistics*:
Depart Ajaccio 08.25; arrive at Corte 10.47. Stroll up the Restonica road, have lunch, and then look around Corte in the afternoon. Depart Corte 17.15; arrive Ajaccio 19.30.
Depart Ponte Leccia 10.11; arrive at Vizzavona 11.39. Walk from the station via the Cascades des Anglais to the Hotel Monte d'Oro for lunch, then return the same way for the train at 16.21; arrive Ponte Leccia 17.52.

Website: cf-corse.corsica

Station telephone numbers:
Ajaccio (04 95 23 11 03
Bastia (04 95 32 80 61
Calvi (04 95 65 00 61
l'Ile-Rousse (04 95 60 00 50
Ponte Leccia (04 95 47 61 29

Lunch suggestions:
Auberge de la Restonica (a 2km walk from Corte)
Hotel Monte d'Oro (a 4km walk from Vizzavona)

Points of interest:
splendid scenery throughout
Gustav Eiffel's Vecchio Viaduct

*These are *approximate* timings; download the latest timetables from the web!

pastures, meander into side-valleys with views to gorges and waterfalls or around promontories at the edge of spectacular cliffs, groan your way up or down through tunnels and overhanging forests of laricio pine, beech and oak. You will see much of the most beautiful scenery of inland Corsica, with mountains rising to over 2600 metres, at the heart of the Regional Natural Park.

Rail enthusiasts were upset when the EU helped to finance the upgrading of Corsica's track and rolling stock. You may find yourself on one of these ultra-modern trains.

Travelling north (sit on the left for the best views):
- **Ajaccio station:** an impressive 19th-century station in a vibrant location at the busy port;
- **Gravona Valley:** on the far side of the river and the T20 is the **Canal de la Gravona**, built to bring water to Ajaccio; it's history was almost as chequered as the railway's;
- leaving **Tavera**, watch on the *right* for a waterfall called the 'Bridal Veil' (**Voile de la Mariée**), at its best in winter and spring;
- **Bocognano:** the train has already climbed over 600m;
- **Vizzavona tunnel:** 4km long — and so straight that from the driver's window light can be seen at the far end;

- **Vizzavona:** at 906m, the highest point of the line, at the foot of **Monte d'Oro** (2389m); crossroads of the **GR20**; also the **Cascades des Anglais** (Walk 5);
- **Tattone**: another fine walking centre, but the train only stops here on request;
- approaching and leaving **Vivario** the train makes two **deep U-bends** where the engineers were unable to pierce tunnels; this is one of the steepest parts of the line; watch for the T20 and the lower stretch of the railway line far below;
- **Vecchio Viaduct:** engineered by Gustav Eiffel; 140m long and 96m high — probably the most exciting part of the route. It's been said that some tour operators were keen to make the viaduct a bungee-jumping site;
- **Venaco**, at the centre of the island (and the Regional Natural Park, founded in 1972); many large houses built by wealthy families in the 19th century;
- **Poggio-Riventosa:** like Tattone, this is a request stop and another fine walking base (see our Walk 6)
- **Corte:** at the confluence of the Tavignano and Restonica gorges, historical capital of the island, university founded by Pasquale Paoli, citadel, access to our Walk 7.

Travelling south (sit on the right for the best views):
Why, you might wonder, do we start the southbound route at Ponte Leccia? It's just to allow you to stay in bed a little longer, since by car you'll reach Ponte Leccia in less time than the train. But you can, if you prefer, catch a convenient train by starting from Calvi at *(about)* 8.20, Ile-Rousse at 8.53 or Bastia at 9.05.

'u trinichellu' **excursion**

- **Ponte Leccia:** the only junction on the line, with two separate tracks (where the line from Calvi comes in);
- **Golo River** (Corsica's most important watercourse) is on the *left*, but crossed just after **Francardo**, with a fine view up the Golo Valley to **Monte Cinto** (2706m) on the *right*.
- **Col San Quilico**: some 350m above Ponte Leccia;
- then see notes opposite, as you reach **Corte**, then **Poggio-Riventosa, Venaco,** the **Vecchio Viaduct, Vivario, Tattone** and **Vizzavona**.

Not a cow or goat on the line, but a penned-in donkey at Tattone. Animals are free to stray onto the tracks, causing delays. Unfortunately they are often killed or have to be put down.

Here are two *panzetta* (Corsican streaky bacon) recipes we've picked up on the island and made at home with great success. Neither is illustrated.

Braised endives with *panzetta* (endives braisées à la panzetta)

Braise the endives in a skillet with the water, sugar, butter, thyme, salt and pepper. Reduce until the endives are slightly caramelised (about 30min), then add the vinegar. Grill the *panzetta* for about 2min on one side, then place it, ungrilled side up, above the endives and grill the lot, still in the skillet, for another 3min.

Beans Corsican-style (haricots à la mode corse)

Again, we make a cheat's version, by using tinned beans. Preheat the oven to 180°C/350°F/gas mark 4.

In a heavy casserole fry together the onions, *panzetta*, carrots and garlic for 5min, stirring constantly. Then add the tomatoes, the beans (haricot or butter beans are equally good) and the bouquet garni, and just cover with cold water. Season and stir together.

Cover the the casserole and cook for 30min. Remove the bouquet garni before serving.

These beans are lovely with grilled sausages!

For the endives: ingredients (for 4 people)
- 8 endives
- 8 thin slices of *panzetta*
- 125 g butter
- 300 ml water
- 50 g caster sugar
- 2 tbsp balsamic vinegar
- salt and pepper
- sprig of thyme

For the beans: ingredients (for 4 people)
- 400 g tinned haricot or butter beans
- 100 g *panzetta*, in small cubes
- 2 tomatoes, peeled, deseeded and chopped
- 2 onions, minced
- 2 carrots, sliced
- 2 cloves garlic, chopped
- 1 bouquet garni
- olive oil

eat
recipes

Chestnut sauerkraut with chestnut beer
(choucroute aux châtaignes à la bière Pietra)

You will need a large, shallow, heavy casserole (diametre about 35 cm/14 in), otherwise divide all the ingredients between two smaller ones (as in the photograph, a casserole for 2-3 people). Preheat the oven to 190°C/375°F/gas mark 5.

Sweat the carrots in a little oil, then drain and set aside. In the same skillet, sweat the minced onion. Mix the onion and chestnuts into the sauerkraut.

Wrap the bay leaves and peppercorns in a little muslin, to make a bouquet garni.

Line the bottom of the casserole with 200 g pork belly slices. Cover with the sauerkraut mixture, and tuck in the muslin bag of bay leaves and peppercorns and the bouquet garni.

Arrange the rest of the pork belly and the carrots on top. Pour over the beer and, if all the ingredients are not covered, add water — or more beer. Bring to the boil on the hob, then place in the oven. It will take a good two hours to cook through.

Remove the bouquet garni, bay and peppercorns. Serve with boiled potatoes, dark country bread and chestnut beer! Or, for a 'meatier' meal, use this dish as an accompaniment to pork, ham or sausages.

Ingredients (for 4 people)
- 600 g bottled sauerkraut, drained)
- 1 onion, peeled and minced
- 200 g prepared chestnuts
- 3 carrots, halved lengthwise
- 1 bouquet garni
- 10 bay leaves
- 10 black peppercorns
- 300 g sliced smoked pork belly
- 500 ml Pietra (chestnut) beer
- 4 tbsp sunflower oil

Public transport: bus and train

The unofficial, private website for buses and trains, **corsicabus.org**, is brilliant and will save you a lot of time searching timetables!

Walk 1*: a) 🚌 Ajaccio—Bonifacio (Corsica Europa Travel, www.corsicaeuropa.com, ✆ 04 95 71 24 64). Year-round departures Mon-Sat from the bus station at Ajaccio's port. Depart Ajaccio 08.30, *change* at Scopetto 11.15, arrive Bonifacio 11.50. Depart Bonifacio 16.40, *change* at Scopetto 16.55, arrive Ajaccio 20.00. **b)** 🚌 Porto-Vecchio—Bonifacio (same operator, but ✆ 04 95 70 13 83). Depart Mon-Sat from rue Pasteur 08.30, 12.00; arrive Bonifacio 30min later. Departs Bonifacio 10.00, 12.45, 17.30
*Jul/Aug departures; *times outside high season usually earlier*

Walk 2: same service as Walk 3. Alight at l'Ospédale and follow the Mare à Mare Sud (see map).

Walk 3: 🚌 Porto-Vecchio—Bavella (Balesi Evasion, www.balesievasion.com, ✆ 04 95 17 50 55). Year-round departures Mon-Fri (also Sat/Sun in Jul/Aug). Departs Porto-Vecchio 07.00, l'Ospédale 07.25; arrives Bavella 08.10. Departs Bavella 17.50, l'Ospédale 18.30; arrives Porto-Vecchio 19.00.

Walk 4: 🚐 Ajaccio—La Parata (city bus No 5). Daily departures (including holidays) from the Place Général de Gaulle; journey time 20min. (Note that from 1/7 to 31/8 services are more frequent; from 1/11 to 31/3 they may be less frequent.) Depart Ajaccio from 07.10 at least hourly until 19.10; depart La Parata 07.20 at least hourly until 19.40.

Walk 5: 🚆 service Ajaccio—Bastia, operated by Chemins de Fer de la Corse (www.cf-corse.corsica; ✆ Ajaccio 04 95 23 11 03, ✆ Bastia 04 95 32 80 61, ✆ Calvi 04 95 65 00 61). Connections from Calvi and l'Ile-Rousse at Ponte Leccia. Following are some low season departures; there are many others; *download an up-to-date timetable!*

public transport

Outbound, Mon-Fri, Sep-Jun

Ajaccio	Vizzavona	Vivario	Venaco	Corte	P. Leccia	Bastia
08.12	09.25	09.41	10.02	10.18	10.56	11.58
Bastia	P. Leccia	Corte	Venaco	Vivario	Vizzavona	Ajaccio
07.54	09.03	09.39	10.01	10.17	10.35	11.43

Return, Mon-Fri, Sep-Jun

Ajaccio	Vizzavona	Vivario	Venaco	Corte	P. Leccia	Bastia
16.35	17.49	18.05	18.20	18.42	19.18	20.21
Bastia	P. Leccia	Corte	Venaco	Vivario	Vizzavona	Ajaccio
16.56	18.01	18.39	18.55	19.11	19.29	20.31

Walk 6: as 5 (b) above: Poggio-Riventosa *(a request stop!)* is 5min north of Venaco

Walk 7: to Corte (as Walk 5 above), then taxi or Line C13 to the Pont de Frasseta (May-Sep *only*); see autocars-cortenais.fr

Walk 8: no suitable public transport (current schedules inconvenient)

Walk 9: departs l'Ile-Rousse 08.00, arrives Ostriconi 08.45, arrives St-Florent 09.30. Autocars Mariani (04 95 65 04 72. *Only* Jul-Aug. departs Bastia at 08.30 Mon, Tue, Thu, Fri; departs 06.35 Wed; Jul/Aug *only*. Sarl Autocars (04 95 36 08 21. Places are limited: book ahead!

Walk 10: as Walk 9 from l'Ile-Rousse.

Walk 11: Calvi—l'Ile-Rousse (as Walk 13)

Walk 12: no suitable public transport; nearest base is Calvi (Walk 11)

Walk 13: Calvi—l'Ile-Rouse, operated by Chemins de Fer de la Corse (www.cf-corse.corsica; as Walk 5 above). Daily 'train-tram' coastal service between Calvi and Ile-Rousse, stopping at all resorts en route. Frequent service in high summer; in shoulder season, typical departures* from Calvi are: 08.00, 09.50, 12.40, 16.00; from l'Ile-Rousse at 09.00, 10.50, 11.50, 13.30, 15.10, 16.05. 19.55.

*Mon-Fri departures; times of departures on weekends vary slightly

As mentioned on page 5, we've been visiting Corsica for many years, first just enjoying the walks in Noel's *Landscapes of Corsica* and later updating that book. Spending so much time on the island would be prohibitively expensive in hotels, so we go self-catering, but usually have a restaurant meal once a day.

After many years as a coeliac, John also became lactose intolerant. Food intolerances are becoming ever more common — or recognised for what they are — and we know *there are a lot of you out there!* Even if you have learned to cope at home, where gluten- and dairy-free foods are now supermarket staples, it can be very daunting to go on holiday overseas. *Will the food in restaurants be safe? Will I be able to buy gluten- and dairy-free foods?*

If you suffer from food intolerance you have probably already learned at home that what initially seems a penance soon becomes a challenge and eventually a joy. We eat far healthier meals now than we did before, with fewer additives. Nowhere is this more enjoyable than around the Mediterranean and on Corsica, where olive oil, fish, tomatoes and 'alternative' grains and flours are basic to the diet. Many, many dishes are *naturally* gluten- and dairy-free.

Of course food intolerances *are* restrictive — in the sense that we have to carry, buy or bake gluten-free breads and sweets, and we always need access to dairy-free 'milk', 'cream', 'yoghurt' and 'butter'. So over the years we've sussed out eating gf, df on Corsica, and it's *so simple.*

EAT GF, DF

EATING IN RESTAURANTS

Common **first courses** are mixed Corsican meats or pâtés, soups, fish and salads, almost all of which are gf, df. The famous *suppa corse* does, however, contain pasta. As this is added at the last minute, you could ask them to leave it out. Fish soups are *not* thickened with flour and very few contain cream — even though they look and taste 'creamy'. Beware of the uniquitous *salade bergère:* this contains cheese (usually warm goats' cheese). Many omelettes feature *brocciu* cheese, but there is no reason why they can't make it without.

The most popular **main courses** are fish and seafood, stews (beef or game), steaks and chops. Sauces, which are *very popular,* usually consist of wine, herbs and garlic, all reduced. If you are a sauce addict, like John, it is safer to *ask* (see inside back flap for help in French, although the staff usually speak English); you are likely to be pleasantly surprised. *Fried* fish is invariably dusted with flour (otherwise it is more difficult to cook), but just *ask:* they are happy to do it for you without flour. Or have grilled filleted fish with the sauce on the side. Most of the restaurants recommended here are family-owned and *know* what is going on in their kitchens!

We are usually too full to have **dessert** but, if you have a sweet tooth, you'll be pleased to know that restaurant chestnut cakes are often 100% gf, df; the same can be said for the chestnut tart at Bavella — just eat the filling. All restaurants offer fruit (including many exotic fruits) for dessert, and some have gf, df chocolate dishes (made with dark chocolate); *ask!*

SELF-CATERING

While many hotels on the island can cater for food intolerances, we discovered the joy of self-catering years ago. What a liberation! Room to swing a cat (or, more likely, chop up a rabbit). Tables where you can spread out your maps and bus timetables. Sofas to loll about on with a good book on a rainy day.

But if we're staying in self-catering for a couple of weeks or more, we *do* treat ourselves to the odd night at an hotel — perhaps at the other end of the island or in the mountains. It's relatively easy to cope for just a night or two, even if they don't have the supplies. They will let you use their fridges (just take a carrier bag or container and label with your name and room number); the non-perishables can stay in your room.

Gf, df shopping

Only the larger Corsican **supermarkets** (Super U, Géant Casino, Leclerc and the like) have separate sections for gluten- or dairy-free products, but they all carry the *naturally* gf flours used on the island like chestnut flour *(farine de châtaigne)* and corn meal for polenta *(semoule de maïs)*. And all have soya milk and delicious soya sweets — sometimes displayed with their non-df equivalents, other times in the *diététique* section, where you may well find soya cream, as well as rice or almond milk. Rice cakes are available everywhere.

There *are* also **health food** shops in the some of the main towns catering for food intolerances (and vegetarians/

vegans). But unfortunately, these tend to go out of business frequently, and we find it is best to rely on the larger firms shown in the panel at the right.

The largest distributor of health foods on the island is **La Roulotte**, with three good self-service outlets. The Bastia branch will also deliver throughout the Balagne but, if you don't speak French, it's best to prepare a list of what you need and get someone else to telephone them. La Roulotte and the largest supermarkets are in shopping centres on main roads, so inconvenient for those without wheels.

It is best to call at a health food shop selling 'bio' products; apart from

---

SOME SHOPS SELLING GF, DF

See locations on their websites

Ajaccio
La Roulotte, Route de Mezzavia (04 95 22 69 47; www.laroulotte-bio.fr
Naturalia, 17 Cours Napoléon (04 95 21 79 65; www.magasins.naturalia.fr
Marché Ajaccio, 7 bd du Roi Jérôme: large stand sells GF (and some DF) baked goods which people rave about; but the owner is coeliac.

Bastia
La Roulotte, N193, Furiani (04 95 34 47 08; www.laroulotte-bio.fr

Calvi
La Vie Claire, 84 rte de Calvi, (04 95 07 83; www.magasins.lavieclaire.com

Corte
La Vie Claire, 7 avenue de la République, (04 95 34 47 08; www.magasins.lavieclaire.com

l'Ile-Rousse
Leclerc, Carrefour de Fogata (see map on page 118) (04 95 63 03 33

Porto-Vecchio
Bodélice, Cacao, Chemin d'Agnarella (04 95 25 96 62; www.biodelice.fr

San Giuliano
La Roulotte, Chemin Tour Caselle (04 95 38 88 84; www.laroulotte-bio.fr

La Roulotte, try Naturalia and La Vie Claire (phone numbers and websites in the panel on page 137). We have also heard that pharmacies will get GF products for you.

Aside from the normal gf, df products you will be looking for, try some other grains and flakes — like Celnat's 'Flocons de Châtaignes Toastés' (toasted chestnut flakes).

Gf, df cooking

We've made all the **recipes** in this book using gluten- and dairy-free ingredients. Basically we just used a 1:1 substitution, and the cooking method was unchanged.

The only problem we ever have is with *frying*, when the recipe calls for a mixture of oil and butter (or just butter). But this was not a problem on Corsica. You can buy 50% sunflower oil spreads from supermarkets or from La Roulotte (look for the 'Rapunzel' brand. Both spread and fry like a dream.

CONVERSION TABLES

Weights		Volume		Oven temperatures		
10 g	1/2 oz	15 ml	1 tbsp			gas
25 g	1 oz	55 ml	2 fl oz	°C	°F	mark
50 g	2 oz	75 ml	3 fl oz	140°C	275°F	1
110 g	4 oz	150 ml	1/4 pt	150°C	300°F	2
200 g	7 oz	275 ml	1/2 pt	170°C	325°F	3
350 g	12 oz	570 ml	1 pt	180°C	350°F	4
450 g	1 lb	1 l	1-3/4 pt	190°C	375°F	5
700 g	1 lb 8 oz	1.5 l	2-1/2 pt	200°C	400°F	6
900 g	2 lb			220°C	425°F	7
1.35 g	3 lb			230°C	430°F	8
				240°C	475°F	9

glossary

MENU ITEMS
à point medium rare
agneau/agnellu lamb
 de lait milk-fed
ail garlic
aïoli mayonnaise with garlic
arête fish bone *(sans arêtes =* filleted)
aromates aromatic spices
artichaut artichoke
asperges asparagus
assiette de plate of
 régionale regional produce
basilic basil
beignet fritter
bleu very rare
blettes Swiss chard
boeuf beef
brocciu ewes'-milk cheese
brochette skewer
calamars squid
canard duck
caneton duckling
carpaccio slivered meat or fish
carré cutlet or chop from best end of neck
cassoulet corse made with lamb
cèpes ceps (porcini-like mushrooms)
champignons mushrooms
châtaignes sweet chestnuts
chevreau kid
choix, au choice of
civet stew
confit preserved
confiture chutney, jam
coppa smoked Corsican meat (see page 8)
coquillages shellfish
coquilles St-Jacques scallops
côte chop, side
coulis thick sauce
crabe crab
croustade de la mer shellfish
croustiallant basically means 'crispy'; in a salad might refer to toast beneath grilled cheese
daube stew
daurade gilthead bream
écrevisses freshwater crayfish
encomets small ilex squids
entrecôte rib steak
farcies stuffed
fiadone lemon-flavoured *brocciu* cake
figatellu pork liver sausage
foie gras goose liver
fruits de mer seafood
gambas giant prawns
girolles mushrooms
grillé grilled
farci stuffed
haricots beans
 — verts green beans
jambon ham
 fumé smoked
langouste spiny lobster
lapin rabbit
légumes vegetables
lièvre hare
loup (de mer) sea bass
miel honey
mignon small (round) piece
morue salt cod
moules mussels
noix nuts
oignon onion
pageot porgy, a sea bream
pain bread
pané breaded
panzetta Corsican streaky bacon (see page 130)
persil parsley
petit small
pignons pine nuts
pistou mixture of garlic, basil and olive oil
poire pear
poireau leek
poisson fish
poivron sweet pepper
porcelet suckling pig
prizuttu Corsican 'prociutto' (see page 8)
raisins grapes
rascasse scorpion fish
rouget red mullet
rouille mayonnaise of olive oil, garlic, chile and saffron
salade salad
 bergère see page 103
 du pecheur salad with seafood
sanglier/cingale wild boar

GLOSSARY

139

sole sole
stuffatu meat stew
tapenade paste of black olives, anchovies and capers
terrine cold 'loaf' of fish, meat or pâté (named for the container in which it is cooked)
tourte sweet-filled pastry case, pie
truite trout
veau veal
volaille poultry

SHOPPING TERMS

apple *pomme*
bacon
  Corsican streaky *panzetta*
basil *basilic*
bass, sea *loup de mer*
bay leaf *laurier*
beans *haricots*
  green *haricots verts*
beef *boeuf*
  cuts:
  fillet *filet*
  marrow *moëlle*
  rump *rumsteak*
  shoulder *paleron*
  sirloin *contre-filet*
  strip loin *faux-filet*
beer *bière*
bread *pain*
bream, gilthead *daurade*
butter *beurre*
cake *gâteau*
cabbage *choux*
cardamon *cardamome*
carrot *carotte*
celery *céleri*
chard, Swiss *blettes*
ceps *cèpes*
cheese *fromage* (*frais* = fresh, *demi-sec* = intermediate stage, *sec* = very mature)
  ewes' milk *brocciu*
  goats'-milk *tomme*
chestnuts, sweet *châtaignes*
chicken *poulet*
chocolate *chocolat*
cider *cidre*
cloves *girofles*
coconut milk *lait de coco*
cod
  fresh *cabillaud*
  salt *morue*
coffee *café*
condiments *condiments*
coriander *coriandre*
corn
  meal *farine de maïs*
  starch *amidon de maïs*
courgettes *courgettes*
crab *crabe*
crayfish *écrevisses*
cream *crème*
cucumber *concombre*
duck *canard*
  breast *magret de canard*
eggs *oeufs*
fennel *fenouil*
figs *figues*
fish *poisson*
flour (wheat) *farine*
  chick-pea *farine de pois chiches*
  corn *farine de maïs*
game *gibier*
garlic *ail*
ginger *gingembre*
goose *oie*
  grease *graisse d'oie*
  liver *foie gras*
grapefruit *pamplemousse*
grapes *raisins*
haddock *aiglefin*
ham *jambon*
  cured *prizuttu*
hare *lièvre*
herbs *herbes*
  local *du maquis*
honey *miel*
ice cream *glace*
juice *jus*
juniper *genièvre* berries
kid *chevreau*
lamb *agneau*
  milk-fed *agneau de lait*
  cuts:
  boneless *sans os*
  cutlets from best end of neck *carré*
  leg (including chump) *gigot*
  loin *filet*
  shoulder *épaule*
leek *poireau*
lemon *citron*
lettuce *laitue*
liver *foie*
lobster *homard*
  spiny *langouste*
mangoes *mangues*
marjoram, Corsican *nepita*
milk *lait*
monkfish *lotte de mer*
mullet, red *rouget*
mushrooms *champignons*
mussels *moules*
mustard *moutarde*
myrtle *myrthe*
nuts *noix*
olive oil *huile d'olive*
onions *oignons*
parsley *persil*
pasta *pâtes*
pastry *pâtisserie*
peanut oil *huile d'arachide*
pear *poire*
peas *pois/petits pois*
pepper (spice) *poivre*
pepper (sweet) *poivron*
pheasant *faisan*
pig, suckling *porcelet*

glossary

When you're in Bastia be sure to visit Maison Mattei on Place St-Nicolas, where all kinds of Corsican speciality foods and wines are beautifully displayed. The building dates from the 1800s and has an interesting history.

pine nuts *pignons*
pork *porc*
  rind *couennes*
  cuts:
  belly *ventrèche*
  boneless *sans os*
  chop *côte*
  cutlet from best
    end of neck *carré*
  escalope *escalope*
  fillet *filet*
  loin *longue*
  shoulder *épaule*
  shoulder, smoked
    lonzu
potatoes *pommes
    de terre*
poultry *volaille*
prawns *crevettes*
  Dublin bay prawns
    langoustines
  giant *gambas*
prunes *pruneaux*
pumpkin *courge*
quail *caille*

rabbit *lapin*
  young *lapereau*
raspberries *framboises*
rice *riz*
rosemary *romarin*
saffron *safran*
sage *sauge*
salmon *saumon*
salt *sel*
  sea *(fleur de sel)*
sausage
  fresh *saucisse*
  dry *saucisson*
  pork liver and
    offal *figatellu*
sauerkraut *choucroute*
scallops *coquilles
  (St-Jacques)*
scorpion fish
  rascasse
sesame oil *huile de
  sésame*
shallots *echalotes*

shellfish *coquillages*
shrimp *crevettes
  grises*
snails *escargots*
sole *sole*
soup *soupe*
soya *soja*
spices *épices*
spinach *épinards*
sugar *sucre*
tarragon *estragon*
tea *thé*
thyme *thym*
tomatoes *tomates*
trout *truite*
tuna *thun*
turbot *turbot,
  turbotin*
turkey *dindon*
  young *dinde*
vanilla pod *gousse
  de vanille*
veal *veau*
  cuts:
  boneless *sans os*

chop *côte*
cutlets *côtelets*
fillet *filet*
filet, smoked *lonzu*
kidneys *rognons*
liver *foie*
loin *carré*
shin, knuckle *jarret*
shoulder *épaule*
sweetbreads *ris*
topside *noix*
vegetables *légumes*
vinegar *vinagre*
  raspberry *de
    framboises*
wine *de vin*
water *eau*
  still *sans gaz*
  sparkling *avec gaz*
watercress *cresson*
wine *vin*
  dry *sec*
  red *rouge*
  white *blanc*

walk & eat CORSICA

bold type: *photograph; italic type: map*

PLACES

Agnone (river) 48, 49, **50**, 51, *52-53*
Ajaccio 6, 8, 125, *126, 127*, 128, 132, 133
 plan *inside front cover*
Anse de Fornali 83, *84*, **85**
Bastia 6, 8, 125, 128, 132, 133, 137, **141**
 plan *inside front cover*
Balagne, la 106, 107, *108-109*, **109, 110**, **114**, 115, *116-117*, **117**, *118*, **119**
Bavella 35, *36*, **39**
 Aiguilles de Bavella **34**, *36*, **38**
 Col de Bavella **34**, 35, *36*, **39**
Boconago *126*, 127
Bonifacio **16**, 17, *18*, **19, 20, 21**, 22
Calanche (near Lumio) *108-109*, **110**
Calvi 95, *96-97*, **98**, 99, 100, 101
Cap Corse **82**, *84*
Capo Pertusato 17, *18*, **19**, *21*, 22
Casanova 60, 61
Cascades d'Aitone 76, 77, 78, **79**
Cascades des Anglais 48, **50**, 51, *52-53*, 125, 128
Cateri 115, *116-117*
Corte 125, *126*, 128, 129
Désert des Agriates **82**, *84*, **85**, 86, **90**, 91, *92-93*
Evisa **76**, 77, 80
Foce, la 49, *52-53*
Foce Alta **26**, 27, *28-29*
Ile-Rousse, l' 106, 115, *118*, **119**, **120**, 121
Lavatoggio 107, *108-109*, 110, 111, 115, *116-117*
Lumio 106, 107, *108-109*, **111**
Monte (mountain) d'Oro 48, 54, 55, *126*, 128
Leonardo 68, *70*
Notre-Dame de la Serra (chapel above Calvi) **94**, 95, *96-97*
Notre-Dame de la Stella (chapel above Lumio) **106**, 107, *108-109*, 110
Occi **106**, *108-109*
Occiglioni **117**, *118*, 119
Ospédale, l' (village, reservoir) *28-29*, **30**, *126*
 Fôret de l'Ospédale **26**, 27, *28-29*, **29**, **30**, 31
Ostriconi, Plage de l' (and Village de vacances) **90**, 91, *92-93*
Parata, la (Pointe de, Tour de) **42**, 43, 44, 45, 46, 47
Poggio-di-Venaco 59, 60, 61, **62**
Poggio-Riventosa 59, 128
Pont de Grotelle 69, *70*, **71**
Ponte Leccia 125, *126, 127*
Punta di a Vacca Morte 27, *28*
Punta Mortella **82**, *85, 86*
Restonica, Gorges de la **68**, 69, *70*, **71**, **72**, **73**, 125
Revellata, la (peninsula) 95, *96-97*, **98**, 99
Riventosa 60, 62
Saint-Florent 83, *84, 85, 86, 87*
Sant' Antonino **114**, 115, *116-117*, **121**
Santo-Pietro-di-Venaco **58**, 60, **62**, 63, **64**
Sentier
 de la Sittelle 77, 78
 des Cascades *52-53*
 des Tafoni 27, *28-9*, **29**
 du Littoral des Agriates **82**, 83, *84*, 87, *86*, *90*, *91*
Sevani 43, 44
Tattone *126*, 128, **129**

142 INDEX

index of places and recipes

Trou de la Bombe (Bavella) 36, **37**, 38
Vecchio River **124**, 125, 128, 129
Viaduct **124,** 125, 128, 129
Venaco 60, 61, 62, **65**, *126*, 128, 129
Vivario *126*, 128, 129
Vizzavona **48,** 49, 52-53, **53,** 125, *126*, 128, 129
Tunnel 54, 55 , 127
Col de **53**, 52-53, **55**, 125

RECIPES

aubergines, stuffed
Bonifacio-style 24-**25**
Porto-Vecchio-style 24
beans Corsican-style 130
beef
stuffatu **103**
boar, wild, stew with ceps **33**
brocciu (ewes'-milk cheese)
cake *(fiadone)* **123**
omelette 25
chestnut
and pork terrine **105**
cake **123**
'petit Napoléon' **89**
tarte **41**
sauerkraut with beer **131**
chicken in curry and coconut milk 66
courgette fritters **47**
duck breast with honey sauce **56**
endives, braised with *panzetta* 130
fiadone (lemon-flavoured cake with *brocciu* cheese) **123**
figs
Corsican fig chutney **32**
veal sauté with prunes and figs **113**
fritters, courgette **47**
lamb
roast leg of, with garlic **74**
stuffatu **103**
mussels
Corsican-style **88**
Provençal-style 88
omelette with *brocciu* (ewes'-milk cheese) 25
panzetta (Corsican streaky bacon)
beans Corsican-style with 130
endives braised with 130
pork
and chestnut terrine **105**
cold platter of Corsican pork **8**
prawns, Dublin Bay *(langoustines)* risotto **104**
prizuttu (smoked ham)
meat stew with *(stuffatu)* **103**
rabbit sautéed with ceps **81**
red mullet Corsican-style **122**
risotto with Dublin Bay prawns **104**
salad
bergère **103**
seafood with citrus vinaigrette **112**
sauerkraut, chestnut, with beer **131**
sea bass grilled with fennel **75**
soup, Corsican *(suppa Corsa)* **102**
stuffatu (meat stew with smoked ham) **103**
suppa Corsa (traditional Corsican soup) **102**
tarte, chestnut **41**
tomato sauce
for aubergines 24
for fritters **47**
trout with pine nuts **57**
veal
cutlets in honey sauce with mushrooms **40**
sauté with prunes and figs **113**
vegetable 'cake' 67

143

walk & eat CORSICA

Third edition © 2025
Published by Sunflower Books
PO Box 36061, London SW7 3WS
www.sunflowerbooks.co.uk

All rights reserved. No part of this publication may be reproduced, stored in a retrieval system, or transmitted by any form or by any means, electronic, mechanical, photocopying, recording or otherwise, without the prior written permission of the publishers.

ISBN 1-85691-567-0

Cover photograph: the Restonica River (Walk 7)

Photographs: John Underwood, Noel Rochford and Shutterstock (pages 48, 58, 76, 82, 106, 127, cover)
Maps: John Underwood, adapted from French IGN maps (1:25,000)
Cookery editor: Marina Bayliss
A CIP catalogue record for this book is available from the British Library.
Printed and bound in England by Short Run Press, Exeter

Before you go ...
log on to
www.sunflowerbooks.co.uk
and click on the '**updates**' tab on the page for *walk & eat Corsica*, to see if we have been notified of any changes to the routes or restaurants.

When you return ...
do let us know if any routes have changed because of road-building, storm damage or the like. Have any of our restaurants closed — or any new ones opened *on the route of the walk*? (Not restaurants in the large towns, please; these books are not intended to be complete restaurant guides!)

Send your comments to info@sunflowerbooks.co.uk